SQUARE-TO-SQUARE GOLF IN PICTURES

SQUARE-TO-SQUARE GOLF IN PICTURES

An illustrated study of
the modern swing techniques

by JIM FLICK
with Dick Aultman

GOLF DIGEST, INC.
Norwalk, Connecticut

Trade Book Distribution by
Simon and Schuster

Copyright © 1974 by Golf Digest, Inc.

Published by
GOLF DIGEST
A New York Times Company

297 Westport Avenue
Norwalk, Connecticut 06856

Book trade distribution by
Simon and Schuster
Rockefeller Center, 630 Fifth Avenue
New York, New York 10020

First Printing

ISBN 0-914178-050-9

Library of Congress Catalog Card Number: 74-77083

Manufactured in the United States of America

CONTENTS

INTRODUCTION

Perhaps the most talked about golf instruction theory of the past 50 years is the Square-to-Square Method. This method first gained widespread public attention in 1970 when Golf Digest published *The Square-to-Square Golf Swing.*

At that time I was editor of *Golf Digest* magazine and I also wrote the book, working closely with several top teachers, especially Jim Flick, head professional at Losantiville Country Club, Cincinnati, Ohio.

In this new book, *Square-to-Square Golf In Pictures,* Jim Flick is the author and I have served as his editor. Flick's primary objective in this new book is to eliminate certain difficulties in learning the method which high handicappers have tended to experience and to better explain how Square-to-Square works for every golfer, regardless of ability. He shows simply and graphically with photographs of top professional stars and average golfers what the Method is and how it can work for you.

I feel the book represents an invaluable pictorial record of the modern golf swing. Drawing largely from the files of *Golf Digest* magazine, Jim and I spent hours and hours over a period of months selecting those photographs, many of them rapid-swing sequences.

The pictures have been carefully selected to clarify exactly what you, the reader, should do and not do. Jim believes that all golfers need clear mental images of what they are trying to accomplish in their swings. The clearer the picture in the pupil's mind, the better his chances are of duplicating that mental picture during the physical act of swinging. Fuzzy swing images produce bad swings. Clear mental pictures eliminate confusion; they even help golfers with poor swings play better.

In the text Jim supplements the photos with advice on HOW to best apply the points made in the photos and WHY they should be applied. At no time does he put words into the mouth of any touring professional, but rather lets the photos themselves show exactly what these model players do in their swings.

Another goal of this book is to make Square-to-Square easier to learn in practice sessions and apply on the course. Jim and I believe that one weakness of much printed golf instruction is that too often it tosses all players into the same hopper, regardless of their age, sex, size and ability. In this book various avenues of learning and application will be suggested for various types of golfers. The final chapter, especially, takes the reader beyond mechanics and tells him how to blend the various parts into a smooth flowing whole.

The original book pointed out that the Square-to-Square Method is designed in part to simplify one's swing by eliminating unnecessary movement. Therefore, it was written primarily for players who already had plenty of MOTION, those who could already swing their arms and turn their bodies freely.

This new book teaches Square-to-Square in a way that still eliminates unnecessary motion yet ADDS freedom of movement WHERE it is needed for those who need it.

At all times the reader will be encouraged to convert the various techniques to his or her own personal sense of feel. Jim believes that the role of the teacher is to tell the student what to do and why to do it. The role of the pupil is to first understand the "why," then

master the "what" through practice and, finally, to "internalize" the feelings of proper execution. He stresses that the best players play their best when they play by feel rather than by conscious mental direction. Jim often says that, "You can never swing your best when you're thinking about HOW to swing."

Another goal of this book is to correct certain misunderstandings about Square-to-Square. The Method, for instance, does not call for the clubface to be looking at the target throughout the swing. Obviously it would take a double- or triple-jointed contortionist to maintain such positioning. Also, some interpreted the first book's reference to a "relatively" upright swing plane as meaning "perfectly" upright. They visualized the clubhead path in the Square-to-Square swing as being identical to that of a moving Ferris wheel, a path on which the clubhead would never leave the target line. Of course it must leave the line, and does in the Square-to-Square swing as Jim explains in the first chapter.

I first met Jim Flick at the 1968 Masters tournament in Augusta, Ga. Our meeting was arranged by the magazine's president, Bill Davis, who had met Jim that winter and studied his massive scrapbook of various golf swing photos, largely dealing with what was then known as the "Square Method."

Golf Digest had published aspects of the Square Method as early as 1954, but no one had ever codified the various pieces into a total method.

Jim and I set out to do just that in an article for *Golf Digest.* After listening to his cogent thoughts for only a few hours, I realized the topic demanded not one article, but rather a series. Later meetings clearly showed that only in book form could the subject be given the full attention it warranted. Thus evolved *The Square-to-Square Golf Swing.*

Though some 80 per cent of that book simply dealt with a presentation of basic, generally accepted swing principles, it created more conversation about the golf swing than, perhaps, any other in the history of the game. It was interpreted—and mis-interpreted—both within the teaching profession and among weekend players from Pinehurst to Tokyo.

Since that time both Jim and I have had ample opportunity to assess the strengths and weaknesses of both the first book and the Method itself. His thinking about Square-to-Square and its application to pupils has been somewhat modified through his teaching of thousands of lessons to "average" golfers, and by his continuous exchanges with fellow teachers, especially Bob Toski and Bill Strausbaugh, with whom he's worked in various teaching seminars conducted by the Professional Golfer's Association (PGA) and the National Golf Foundation.

In this book Jim also includes some methodology that differs from that of the first book. It reflects an evolution in the Method that is to be expected when the mind behind it is as inquiring and open to change as Jim Flick's.

My own view of the golf swing in general and Square-to-Square in particular also has been broadened, largely through work on subsequent books with Toski *(Touch System for Better Golf)* and California professional Eddie Merrins *(Swing the Handle, Not the Clubhead),* and giving thousands of lessons at Golf Digest instruction schools conducted by Toski and the eminent British instructor, John Jacobs.

Golfers who read the first Square-to-Square book will find that in this one Jim re-affirms the basic principles and goals of the original. Indeed, one goal of this book is to review Square-to-Square concepts and techniques, not only to refresh the minds of those who read the original text, but also to introduce the Method to new readers.

I hope you will read and re-read this book carefully. I feel strongly that Jim's words deserve maximum attention from all of the world's truly devoted golfers.

Dick Aultman
Westport, Conn.
December, 1973

1.
WHAT SQUARE-TO-SQUARE IS AND WHAT IT DOES

Essentially, golf is a game of chase. The quarry is perfection—more elusive than the quickest jackrabbit, the sliest fox, the most transient state of bliss.

Ponder the problems of striking a golf ball perfectly. The ball itself is barely over 1½ inches in diameter. The clubface is only slightly larger. It is affixed to the end of a flexible shaft some 36-43 inches in length. The clubhead may be moving over 100 miles per hour at impact.

For a perfect shot to occur, this clubhead must be moving straight down the target line at the split-second it contacts the ball. The clubface must be looking in exactly the same direction that the clubhead is moving. The clubhead must be at just the right height in relation to the ball—not too high, not too low. It must be moving at the exact speed required —not one mile per hour too fast or too slow —to move the ball a specific distance.

No wonder we so seldom make even a near-perfect shot. No wonder it thrills us to the bottom of our spikes when we do.

Strictly speaking, there are two basic ways to move an object. You can stand in front of it and pull it, or you can stand behind it and push it or shove it.

In golf, however, we stand alongside the ball. Part of our body is ahead of it and part is behind. Thus the golf swing can—and does —involve both pulling and some combination of pushing, shoving and throwing.

The premise of Square-to-Square is that you are more likely to produce the perfect impact I've just described if you PULL your club into position during the early stages of your forward swing than if you THROW, PUSH or SHOVE it.

By improving your ability to pull the club into position, you will (1) add distance because your clubhead will move through the ball faster and (2) increase your accuracy because your clubhead will remain on the target line and face down that line longer through impact.

The easiest position from which to pull

the club is the so-called "Square Position." This position is one in which the back of your left hand, wrist and forearm form a straight-line relationship. It is called the Square Position simply because the pulling action that can be applied from it gives you your best chance of contacting the ball squarely. As the original book pointed out, if you establish this straight-line Square Position either at address or early in your backswing, and maintain it to near the finish of your forward swing, you are, in fact, swinging from Square to Square.

Pulling the clubshaft is simpler if you use the muscles that are on the left side of your body because those muscles are in front of the object being pulled. During the forward swing this involves (1) the last three fingers of your left hand, which are in front of the clubshaft, (2) your left arm, which is connected to this hand and (3) your legs. Pushing, shoving or throwing the club would involve using muscles of (1) your right hand because it is behind the clubshaft, (2) your right arm and (3) your shoulders.

Most golf swings—I'd say about 99.9 per cent—involve too much pushing, shoving

or throwing of the club early in the forward swing. Invariably the right hand dominates the left and the shoulders dominate the legs. In short, right-handers rely largely on their right hand and arm, left-handers on their left. This is only natural when you think of the many things you do every day with your dominant hand, arm and shoulder—eating, shaving, writing, turning doorknobs, washing windows, polishing the car, even brushing your teeth. Put a muscularly dominant hand, arm and shoulder BEHIND a clubshaft which you're trying to swing forward and, instinctively, they will try to assume control.

The results are all too familiar—slicing, pulling, hooking, fat shots, topped shots, even shanks. All result from over-controlling the club with the right hand and/or the right arm and shoulder muscles early in the forward swing. Also, throwing the club with the right hand often wastes centrifugal force so that the clubhead actually decelerates into the ball.

I will have much more to say about these problems and how to cure them in later chapters. Now I merely want to establish that the main goal of the Square-to-Square

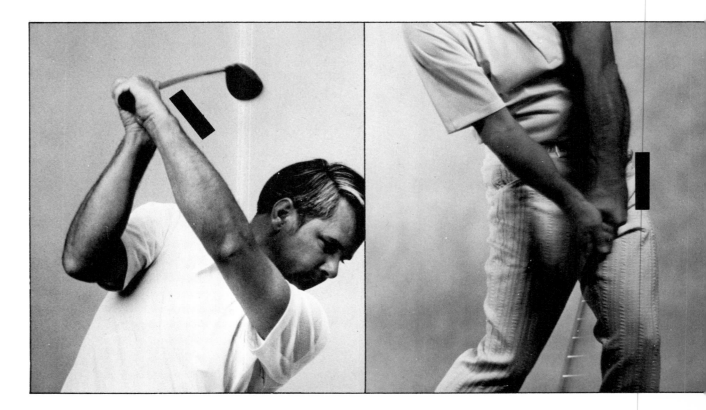

Method is to help you minimize the role played by your right hand, arm and shoulders, and to increase the influence of your left side—hand, arm and legs. Though golf is a bilateral game in which both sides of your body must play a part, the Square-to-Square Method is designed to make you more a puller of the golf club, to give your weaker, less-developed parts an equal billing so that you can strike the ball squarely more often and with increased clubhead speed.

Again, the main reference point in the Square-to-Square swing is the so-called "Square Position," in which the back of your left hand, wrist and forearm form a straight-line relationship, with no inward cupping or outward bowing at the back of the wrist.

Though the Square-to-Square Method does increase your chances of facing the clubhead down the target line during impact, in no way do I mean to imply that the clubface looks at the target throughout the entire swing. Actually the clubhead rotates about 90 degrees as you make your backswing turn, and then about 180 degrees in the opposite direction during your entire forward swing (see photos of Johnny Miller on pages 16 to 19).

I would also like to clarify that while the Square-to-Square Method does increase the span in which the clubhead is moving along the target line through impact, this is not to say that it never leaves this line. As in all golf swings, the clubhead moves to the golfer's side of his target line fairly early in the backswing, remains on this side until near impact and then returns to the golfer's side shortly thereafter.

The act of moving into the Square Position early in the backswing is not designed solely to set the clubshaft into a relationship with your hands from which you can readily PULL, rather than THROW, it during your forward swing. It also serves to establish left-hand dominance, to break down the seemingly innate tendency to over-control the club with the right hand, arm and shoulder area.

Square-to-Square is a total method. Each part—grip, setup, backswing, etc.—fits together with each other part to produce a swing designed to maximize left-side control. Each part, once mastered, makes it simpler to accomplish the other parts. The book also presents Square-to-Square as a "model" method. Some readers may not find it possible to master every one of its parts, but the more parts you can adopt without sacrificing that vital ingredient, freedom of motion, the closer you will come to achieving the perfection I mentioned at the start of this chapter.

The "Square" position

This is the Square Position in which the back of the left hand, wrist and forearm form a straight-line relationship, shown here at the top of the swing, at impact and near the finish of the swing. This is the ideal position for applying a pulling force on the clubshaft early in the downswing and maintaining left-hand control throughout and is a distinctive feature of what we call the Square-to-Square golf swing.

11

1   2   3   4

Pulling vs. throwing

The overriding purpose of the Square-to-Square Method is to produce a swing in which the club is largely PULLED, instead of THROWN or SHOVED, during the downswing. Professional Johnny Miller (top row on these and following six pages) uses his legs, left arm and the last three fingers of his left hand to produce this pulling action.

In contrast, the 18-handicap amateur shown in the bottom photos largely throws the clubhead back to the ball with his right hand and arm. This right-hand throwing action forces his wrists to uncock prematurely in his downswing (photos 6-9) so that he releases clubhead speed too soon and loses distance. It also breaks down the back of his left wrist near impact (photos 12-14) so that his clubhead lifts abruptly just past impact. It doesn't remain at ball level long enough to assure accurate contact consistently.

In photos 1-6 we see Miller swinging the club back

and up with the last three fingers of his left hand, his "pulling hand," and his left arm, his "pulling arm," controlling the club. The amateur, however, picks the club up with his right hand and arm thus giving control of the club over to his "throwing hand" and "throwing arm."

Miller begins his downswing (photos 6-8) with his left knee sliding to his left while the amateur relies largely on his right hand and arm to start the club back to the ball (photos 6-8). By pulling with his legs and his left arm and hand Miller retains his wrist cock later in his downswing (photos 6-8) while the amateur releases his very quickly. Note that Miller's left knee leads everything else throughout his forward swing and his pulling hand and arm lead the clubhead into the hitting area, a classic example of left-side control.

9   10   11   12

13   14   15   16

1   2   3   4

Pulling vs. shoving

Again we see professional Johnny Miller (top photos) demonstrating Square-to-Square principles that result in a high degree of pulling force on the clubshaft during the downswing. In contrast, the 11-handicap golfer in the bottom photos largely shoves or pushes the club back and through the ball. Shoving or pushing results from "top heaviness" wherein the shoulders rather than the legs lead and dominate the forward swing. Pulling with the legs, left arm and last three fingers of the left hand during the downswing helps keep the clubhead moving ALONG the target line longer through impact and thus increases chances of making square contact. Shoving throws the clubhead ACROSS the line from outside to inside during impact. This path

either (1) drives the ball low and left or (2) slices it to the right with a glancing blow if the player has compensated for his outside-inside clubhead path by opening the clubface.

Shoulder tension that leads to shoving often begins at address. Note in photo 1 how Miller's arms hang freely while the amateur's extend stiffly. Miller can swing his arms back and up freely during his backswing (photos 1-7) while the amateur must rely on a large hip turn to get his club moving away from the ball. This stiffens and deactivates his right leg so that later he must shove with his shoulders instead of pull with his legs and left arm during his forward swing.

Note in photos 7-9 how Miller's active legwork and

| 5 | 6 | 7 | 8 |

left hand-arm control pull his right elbow into his side. He can swing his clubhead back to the ball from inside to along his target line and drive the ball forward (photos 13-14). The amateur's shoulder shove throws his elbow away from his side (photos 7-9) so that his clubhead swings too far outside before impact and then quickly inside after. In photo 14 we see his clubhead moving quickly around to his left while his ball slices to the right. He's subconsciously compensated for the impending shot to the left by opening his clubface to the right.

   Two misconceptions about the Square-to-Square swing are that (1) the clubhead never leaves the target line and (2) the clubface always faces the target throughout the swing. The error in such thinking is clearly shown in the swing of Miller which is Square-to-Square as defined in the text and shown in the photos of Jack Nicklaus on pages 20 and 21. Note that Miller's clubhead does leave the line, first during his takeaway and later just past impact, and that his clubface looks squarely at the target only at address and during impact.

13   14   15   16

Square Position is ideal for pulling

The ideal position for applying pulling force to the clubshaft, instead of a throwing or a shoving force, is one in which the back of the left hand, wrist and lower forearm form a straight-line relationship. Here we see Jack Nicklaus in this straight-line relationship at various points in his swing. This relationship is called the "Square Position" because the pulling force that it encourages allows a player to apply his clubhead squarely to the ball more frequently than will a throwing or shoving force. The term Square-to-Square stems from this Square Position, the key feature of the Method. Golfers who establish the Square Position either at address or early in the backswing and who retain it throughout most of their follow-through are thus swinging "Square-to-Square." Neither Nicklaus nor the many other golfers whose swings have this characteristic necessarily describe their own swings in terms of Square-to-Square, but as these photographs clearly show, the Square Position is a noticeable feature.

2.

THE SQUARE-TO-SQUARE GRIP

The way you hold your golf club greatly influences how you actually swing. Your grip is comparable to an apple's core. A rotten core can spread its sour taste throughout the apple. A poor grip certainly sours your chances for a sweet golf swing.

While a good grip is important in the success of any type of swing, it plays a particularly vital role in the Square-to-Square swing.

In any swing the grip should unify the hands so they work together. It should be firm enough to control the club, but not so firm that it stifles free swinging. It should consistently square the clubface to the target line during impact.

In the Square-to-Square swing, your grip must not only accomplish these goals but also establish a certain amount of left-side control. A proper Square-to-Square grip puts control of the club largely in the last three fingers of your left hand. It is this control that, if maintained during your swing, helps you pull rather than throw the club into proper position for square impact.

First I'll talk about how to position your hands on the club; next I'll discuss grip pressure.

There is a certain positioning of the hands that we call the Square-to-Square grip because it pre-sets the back of your left hand, wrist and lower forearm in the straight-line Square Position before you actually swing. You may find this grip uncomfortable at first. It may be different from your present grip. Therefore, I'll not only present the Square-to-Square grip, but also point out the factors that you should consider in deciding whether to assume it at this time or first adopt an intermediate grip.

The Square-to-Square grip is one in which your palms more or less face each other and align with the clubface. Thus both palms are relatively "square" to the target line. If there is to be any departure from this palms-facing, clubface-aligned relationship, it should be that the palm of your right hand faces a

The Square-to-Square grip

Golfers who hold the club with (1) their palms facing and (2) more or less aligned with the clubface and (3) with the back of their left hand, wrist and lower forearm in the straight-line Square Position have a Square-to-Square grip. The photos here show Professional Dave Hill approximating such a grip. Readers who do not already have a Square-to-Square grip should consult the text of this chapter for individual guidance on whether they should try to master it immediately or work toward it in gradual steps.

You can establish a Square Position during the backswing

Many professionals do not use the Square-to-Square grip of Dave Hill shown on the preceding page. Here are two who do not—Bruce Crampton and Lee Trevino. Note the slight inward cupping at the back of the left wrist in each of the top photos. Like most pros, however, both Crampton and Trevino do move into the straight-line Square Position during the backswing (middle photos) and retain it through impact (bottom photos).

smidge more skyward. Most players run into trouble if their right hand tends to crawl over the thumb of their left. This gives over too much control of the club to the thumb and forefinger of the right hand, which in turn activates the top-side muscles—the "throwing" muscles—of the forearm.

In the Square-to-Square grip, the thumb of your left hand extends down the top of the clubshaft, or slightly right of top, so that the back of this hand also aligns more or less parallel with the clubface and thus is also square to the target line. This positioning is ideal for swinging Square-to-Square because in placing your left hand, wrist and lower forearm more or less in the Square Position before you start your backswing, you can sense your impact position as you grip the club.

Unfortunately, this positioning of the hands has been labeled a "weak" grip. The so-called "strong" grip finds the back of the golfer's left hand and the palm of his right hand looking more skyward than down the line.

I submit that these labels are misleading and should be reversed. To me, a strong grip is one that allows the hands to swing through the impact area without the back of the left wrist collapsing and cupping inward. When this collapsing occurs, the clubface becomes misaligned and the clubhead moves off the target line too soon.

I feel that the grip I've described as being ideal is actually strong, not weak, because it is less likely to allow the left wrist to collapse before or during impact. The so-called "strong" grip, on the other hand, often allows the back of the left wrist to collapse inward at the top of the backswing. This opens the clubface. Then, to square the clubface by impact, the golfer must throw the club early in his forward swing with the right hand. This flicks the clubhead at the ball and breaks down the left wrist prior to, or during, impact. A sharp hook or a pull-slice usually results.

Thus, the grip that aligns the palms with the clubface is really stronger than the so-called "strong" grip.

Should you employ this Square-to-Square grip immediately or should you move to it gradually over a period of time and practice? I've found that this depends on three things: (1) how long and how much the pupil has played with his or her present positioning of the hands, (2) how great the variation of this present positioning is from the aligned grip and, most importantly, (3) how much time the student can spend practicing to develop familiarity with the new grip. Unless you have played relatively little golf, or unless your hands position is already close to being aligned with the clubface, I suggest you make the transfer gradually. A major change all at once probably will feel foreign and uncomfortable. It may produce mental

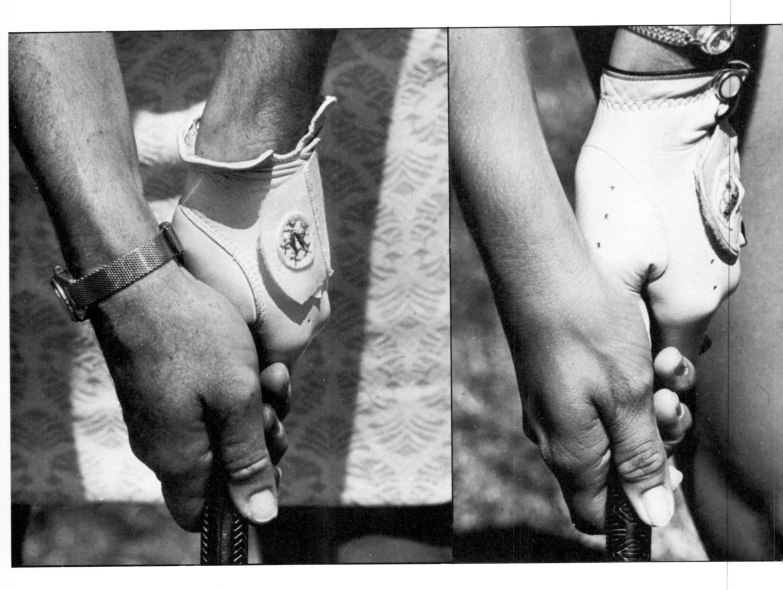

"Strong" vs. "weak"

Contrary to popular belief, many women do not need a so-called "strong" grip—hands positioned well to the golfer's right on the club—as an aid in helping them square the clubface by impact. Nor do all strong men play their best with a so-called "weak" grip—hands turned well to their left. Examples above (left to right) show women professionals Susie Berning and Laura Baugh with the "weak" grips often reserved only for strong men and Billy Casper and Jack Nicklaus with relatively "strong" grips long advocated for women players. The text in this chapter and the photos on page 29, tell and show how an apparent "strong" grip can actually produce a weak impact position. In short, there is some leeway in hand positioning—a 100 per cent Square-to-Square grip is not mandatory for applying a pulling force to the clubshaft.

tension and perhaps affect your alignment and your swing adversely.

I'd like to make one very important point about HOW you assume your grip, regardless of WHAT grip you are using. As you grasp the clubshaft in your left hand simply curl the last three fingers inward and upward toward your palm. This will firmly lodge the shaft against the heel pad. Do not thereafter wrap your hand and wrist over the top of the shaft. This additional movement would activate the muscles of your thumb and forefinger and the top of your forearm. In the Square-to-Square swing the opposite muscles—those of the last three fingers of your left hand, and the UNDERSIDE of your left forearm—should

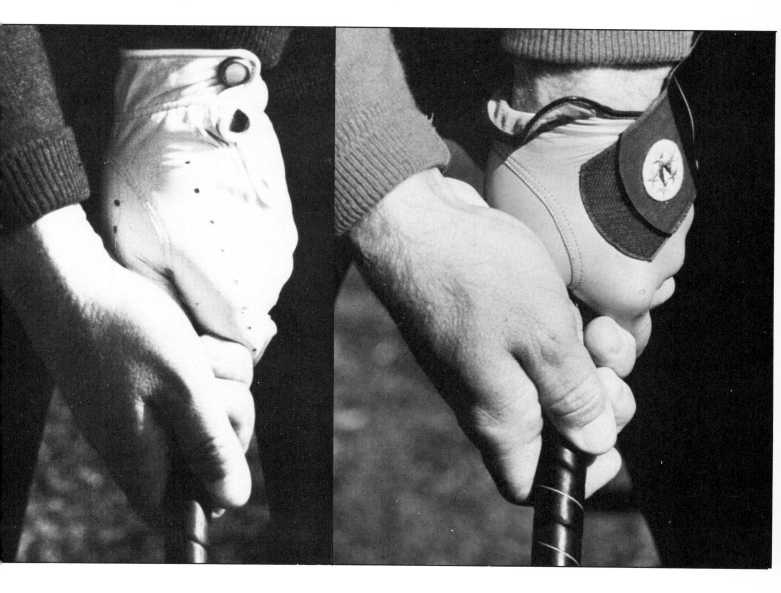

dominate. Turning the left hand over will also encourage your left elbow to move away from your side, a tendency that will frustrate free swinging.

No matter how you grip the club, I think you should position your arms and hands so you do not feel any tension in the muscles that run up the top of your forearms. Arching your wrists upward to an extreme produces such tension. So does dropping your hands extremely low.

How firmly should you grip the club? I feel that light is better than tight. Too much grip pressure in either hand creates arm and shoulder tension that stifles freedom of arm movement. Once proper grip position has

been established the most important goal is to maintain a constant but gentle grip pressure throughout the swing.

One goal of the Square-to-Square swing is to minimize the control exercised on the clubshaft by the right hand. There are two primary danger points to be aware of at address—(1) strong pressure in your right hand, (2) too much pressure in the right thumb and forefinger and (3) stiffening pressure with the right arm, especially in the area around the elbow. All of these pressures create tension that cannot easily be broken down. This makes it almost impossible to arrive at a correct folding of the right wrist and elbow during the backswing. Too much

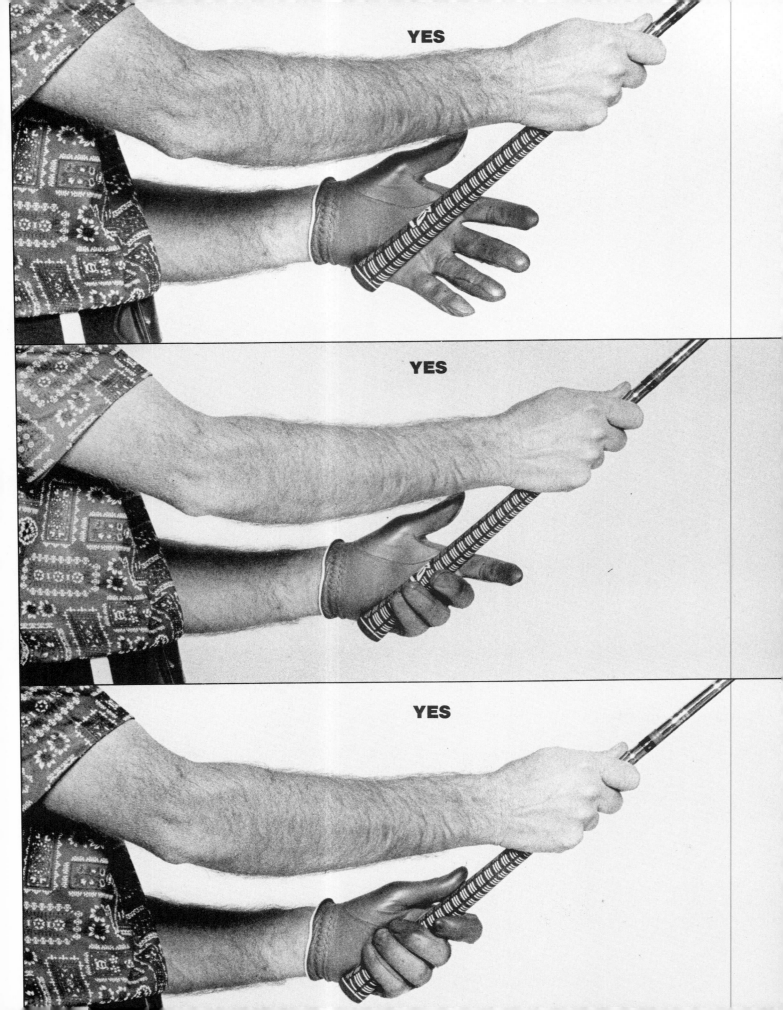

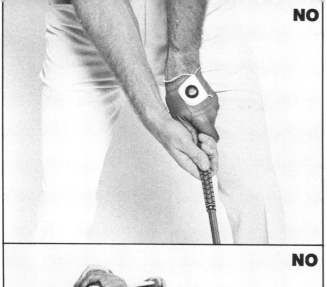

NO

NO

right-hand grip pressure also increases tension in the area of your right shoulder. This tension can shorten your backswing severely and cause you to shove the club back to the ball with this shoulder and arm, instead of pulling it down with your legs and your left arm and hand.

Throughout the Square-to-Square swing, you should control the clubshaft primarily with the last three fingers of your left hand. As you assume your grip, you should identify this feeling of control. You should sense that these three fingers are lightly pressuring the clubshaft against the palm of your left hand. You should not squeeze it tightly, just firmly enough to let you know that these fingers are in command.

You will also need just enough pressure joining your hands so that they will not move apart as you swing. I suggest you accomplish this by gently nudging the heel pad of your right hand forward—toward the target— against the thumb pad of your left hand. This nudging not only joins your hands, but it also reduces the tendency to throw the club with the fingers of your right hand. You should keep the pressure between these pads constant but gentle throughout your swing. Again, however, your main pressure point— both at address and throughout your swing— should be in the last three fingers of your left hand, forcing the clubshaft against the palm.

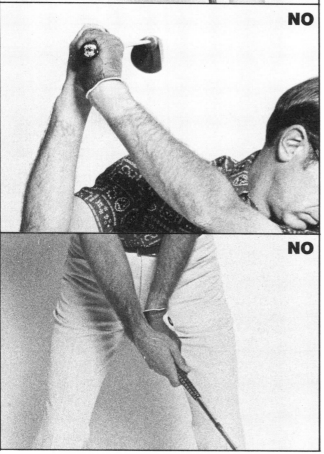

NO

Gripping procedure

Throughout the Square-to-Square swing, the clubshaft must be controlled largely by the last three fingers of the left hand. First, place the clubshaft across the palm of your left hand and under the heel pad (top photo at left). Lock the shaft against this pad by merely curling these fingers firmly upward toward your palm (middle photo). Finally, "trigger" your forefinger lightly under the clubshaft and lay your thumb gently down the top (bottom photo).

It is important that you merely close your last three fingers around the club. Do not thereafter wrap your palm and wrist over the top of the shaft (top photo above) because   activates muscles on the top side of your forearm and this weakens control with the last three fingers. It encourages fanning the clubface open during the backswing and at the top (middle photo) and a violent throwing action on the forward swing to square it by impact (bottom photo).

Bad grips stifle free swinging

Two examples of how a bad grip can adversely influence one's swing. The 36-handicap golfer in the top photos holds the club with his right palm facing upward instead of toward the target. This positions his thumb on top of the shaft in a strong position to throw the clubhead back to the ball with his right hand instead of pulling it with the last three fingers of his left. Normally this right-hand throw would cause him to hook badly to his left, were he to allow his arms and hands to freely rotate counterclockwise through the hitting area. He avoids the hook by avoiding the rotation. The result is a highly inhibited, over-controlled swing. The ball goes fairly straight, but not very far.

The 11-handicap player in the bottom photos also inhibits his forward swing because of bad gripping. His problem is too much grip pressure. This pressure creates arm and shoulder tension that stifles the full build-up and release of clubhead speed that results from swinging the arms freely with a relatively light grip pressure. Over-concern about distance frequently causes undue grip pressure that actually shortens shots.

3.

SETTING UP SQUARE-TO-SQUARE

At this point I'd like to give you a two-question quiz.

Question No. 1: As you address the ball, do you feel:

1. Slight tension or awareness in your legs and knees, but not in your arms and shoulders?
2. Tension in your arms and shoulders, but not in your legs?
3. Somewhat tense all over?
4. Generally relaxed all over?

Hopefully you selected Answer No. 1, but don't be discouraged if you didn't. Most golfers I see are either too relaxed in the legs, too tense in the arms and shoulders or too tense over-all as they prepare to swing. Those of you who selected Answer No. 4 are not in an ideal situation, but not so bad off as if you chose No. 2 or No. 3.

Question No. 2: Do you first aim your clubface behind the ball and then adjust your stance and body alignment, or do you set up first and aim second?

Hopefully you aim first and then align yourself according to the direction the clubface is looking.

Perhaps this is the first time anyone has ever asked you such questions. Perhaps you've never thought about how you feel as you stand over the ball or about your setup procedure. Most golfers give too little thought to how they aim the clubface and set up to the ball.

This is unfortunate. Without question, the way you PREPARE to swing directly determines HOW you swing. I would say that 999 golfers out of every 1,000 hinder their chances of making a good swing to some degree because they mis-aim the club and/or set up to the ball incorrectly.

Let's say you address the ball with "dead legs" and tense arms and shoulders. I seriously doubt that from this starting position you could swing your arms back smoothly and freely and build up full power with a full backswing turn. I doubt that you could swing forward with your legs leading the way,

Square-to-Square setup (frontal view)

Tommy Bolt's model golf swing results largely from his excellent address position. On these pages and the two that follow we show Bolt both at address and at impact so that the reader can see how closely he relates the former to the latter. The Square-to-Square ideals highlighted in the photos are elaborated upon in the text of this chapter.

Head back,
over right knee.
Chin turned
toward right shoulder

Right side
lower than left

Right knee flexed
inward slightly

Most of weight
inside ball
of right foot

Hands lead
clubhead slightly

Left knee
leads shoulder

2

Back straight

Arms hang freely

Forward bending
from hips
puts eye-line
outside hands

Knees flexed,
legs "alive"

Weight toward
balls of feet

pulling your arms and the clubshaft into position for releasing maximum centrifugal force into the ball. Shoulder tension would cut off your backswing and dominate your downswing. Your lazy legs would have little chance to pull your arms and clubshaft forward. They would follow, not lead, your shoulders.

This is just one instance of how your setup determines how you swing. In this chapter I will tell and show you many examples. As you read, please bear in mind the general premise and goal of Square-to-Square. The premise: that you can swing your clubhead down the line and at ball level longer and faster through impact if you increase your ability to pull, instead of throw, shove, or push, the club early in your downswing. The goal: to achieve this pulling of the club by increasing the influence of your left hand on the clubshaft, your left arm and your legs, while reducing the role of your right hand—call it your "throwing hand"—your right arm and your shoulders.

Aiming the clubface

Probably 90 per cent of the world's golfers do not aim the clubface at their target. I know this is hard to believe, but it's true. The seemingly simple act of squaring the clubface to the target line really isn't all that simple. Most of us can stand behind the ball, face

down the target line and readily visualize a line from the target to the ball. Unfortunately, this line becomes distorted once we step alongside the ball and try to square our clubface on target. Also, we tend to compensate for swing deficiencies by mis-aiming the clubface. The slicer, for instance, aims left, which sometimes helps him keep the ball in play. But aiming left fails to correct the basic swing error that caused the slicing. It merely ingrains it deeper.

Most right-handed golfers aim the clubface to the right of target but some aim it left. Whatever the pattern of mis-aiming may be, it demands some sort of compensation and over-control during the swing to square the clubface and move the clubhead along the line through impact. Those who aim to the right must somehow swing or turn the clubhead back to the left—toward the target —prior to impact. Generally this is done with the right shoulder shoving or pushing, or the right hand throwing. The legs, left arm and left hand have little chance to pull on the clubshaft during the downswing. A weak pull-slice usually results.

One way to improve your ability to aim the clubface properly is by using an "intermediate target," a technique employed by many professionals, including Jack Nicklaus. First, stand behind the ball so that it is between you and the target as you face down the line. Visualize your line of flight. Then select a spot

Square-to-Square setup (target view)

Tommy Bolt assumes a square address position with his knees, hips and shoulders all aligned parallel to the target line. Note other Square-to-Square setup ideals highlighted on photos at left and on preceding page.

on that line a few feet in front of the ball. Concentrate solely on the line from the ball to the spot. Aim your club so that the two vertical lines on the clubface, if extended forward along the ground, would parallel the line from the ball to the spot. Since the intermediate target is relatively close at hand, you'll find it relatively simple to square the clubface to it accurately. Just as it's easier to aim a three-foot putt than a 60-footer, it's easier to aim at the spot you've selected on the target line than at the distant target.

Then adjust your stance and body alignment square to the clubface. Align yourself parallel to the line from the ball to the spot. Excellent players square themselves to the clubface. Others aim the clubface according to how they've already aligned their feet and bodies.

The process of selecting the intermediate target also helps funnel your vision and orientation towards a positive target. Your mind is first on the target itself and then on the spot. You block out visions of sand traps, out-of-bounds areas and other pitfalls. Your thinking and your swing will become more positive, more target-oriented and less ball-oriented, especially if you concentrate on swinging through the ball and driving it over the spot.

Setting up

The photos and captions in this chapter highlight the various aspects of a proper address position. Here is how these various setup positions help you attain the goals of Square-to-Square.

1. Play the ball forward. If you play the ball about opposite your left heel on all normal shots you will increase your ability to create lower body motion toward the target. To avoid fat shots you'll be forced to develop your legs and learn to use them as leaders in your forward swing. You'll tend to swing THROUGH the ball. Most people play the ball too far back in their stance. They do so because this positioning allows them to make contact even though they swing down with their arms before their legs, a sequence that would otherwise cause them to stick the clubhead into the ground behind the ball. At a recent Golf Digest instruction school I found that 28 of 32 pupils played the ball too far back. The farther back you play the ball, the more you will chop AT it. You become "ball-bound." This creates a subconscious anxiety that produces over-control of the club, rather than free swinging of the arms. Teeing the ball high also encourages free swinging "through," not "to," and leading with your legs.

2. Set most of your weight inside the ball of your right foot. The original Square-to-Square text called for slightly more weight on the left foot than on the right, a distribution long advocated by players and teachers alike. In recent years I've come to question this accepted principle. After viewing thousands of feet of film and watching thousands of swings by players of various abilities, I now feel that about 60-70 per cent of your weight should be resting on the inside of the ball of your right foot, with the rest on the inside of the ball of your left foot.

One reason I changed my thinking was because I found that too much weight on the left foot can cause what we call a "reverse pivot." During the backswing the player shifts weight toward, instead of away from, the target. During the downswing he reverses this weight shift. He transfers weight onto his right foot in a "fall-back-and-fire" movement.

Others who set up with most of their weight on the left foot overshift during the backswing as they turn away from the target. In attempting to transfer weight onto the right foot their right knee sways out away from the target. Their weight moves to the outside of this foot to the point that they cannot recover and slide weight back onto the left foot at the start of the downswing.

Both the reverse pivot and the overshift usually produce a lateral swaying instead of a proper turning of the body.

The reverse pivot can also cause your shoulders to turn on a too upright plane. This over tilting binds your shoulders and upper body so that you cannot swing your arms fully and freely.

The overshift causes a lateral swaying away from the target during your backswing and either a compensatory sway toward the target or a further falling back during the forward swing.

Ideally you should set up with both knees slightly flexed and cocked a bit toward the target, parallel to the target line. But be careful you do not open your hip alignment to the left in doing so. This positioning, with your knees cocked forward and your weight largely on the inside of the ball of your right foot allows you to make a full, free backswing with little or no additional shifting of weight away from the target. Almost any and all weight shifting you must make during your swing will be forward, toward the target during your forward swing. Instead of two weight shifts back and forward which require a finer sense of timing, you'll need only one. And it will be in the direction you're driving the ball.

3. Your legs should feel alive and springy. As you address the ball they should already feel ready to slide forward at the start of your forward swing, ready to PULL your arms and club through impact. With your weight largely on the balls of your feet and your knees slightly flexed you should be able to tap your heels. Weight on the balls of your feet puts you in the "athletic" position, like a swimmer ready to push off the side of the pool or like a baseball outfielder ready to move with the crack of the bat or a basketball player on defense ready to shift like a cat to either side.

4. Your arms and shoulders should feel soft. While the swimmer's legs are springy as he prepares to dive forward, his arms hang limp. You may see him shake his hands and arms several times to loosen his shoulder muscles. He's trying to eliminate any tension that might restrict his stroke once he's in the water. You should seek this same relaxed softness in your arms and shoulders as you prepare to swing the golf club. Later I'll stress the need for freedom of arm movement and reduced shoulder tension in your swing. Suffice it for now to stress that at address you should strive to combine the springiness in your legs with a relaxation in your arms and shoulders. The only tension you should feel, apart from in your legs, is that slight pressure in the last three fingers of your left hand lodging the clubshaft against the heel pad.

5. Bend forward from your hips with your back fairly straight. For your legs to lead your shoulders in your forward swing you need some "separation" between your legs and upper body. This separation is best established at address by bending forward from your hips and letting your arms hang freely. Overreaching for the ball produces too much tension in your arms and shoulders, and thus stifles freedom of movement. Slouching forward with your back bent and your head hanging down has the same

tension-producing effect since you must lift the club with your arms and shoulders during your backswing.

Study the photos on pages 34 and 39 and note the posture of these fine players at address. You'll achieve a similar posture if you follow this simple procedure.

First, stand upright so that you get a side view of yourself in a mirror. With your legs still straight, bend forward slightly FROM YOUR HIPS. Don't slouch or bend your neck downward. Continue bending from the hips only until your eyes are looking at the spot where your ball would normally be positioned. As you bend forward, suck your lower abdomen in and let your buttocks protrude. Let your arms droop. Once you can see the ball position, stop bending. Flex your right knee slightly forward, toward the left knee. Finally, move your hands together in front of you as if you were gripping the club.

If you've followed this drill carefully, your image in the mirror should be similar to that of the players on these pages. Your rear end should protrude slightly. Your lower back should be straight. Your arms should hang so that your hands appear below your neck or chin, not reaching out beyond your eyes.

6. Align your shoulders, hips and knees parallel to your target line. In the Square-to-Square swing, you'll recall, we seek to move the clubhead along the target line through impact. Your success or failure in producing

Excellent address positions

Outstanding setups shown here include those of (clockwise from top-left) Ben Crenshaw, Tom Weiskopf, Gary Player and Bruce Crampton. Readers will note in these players the following Square-to-Square ideals: (1) ball played well forward, golfer's head well back; (2) right side lower than left; (3) legs alive with knees flexed; (4) arms hang freely; (5) back straight; (6) bent from hips so hands fall inside eye line; (7) weight largely on inside of ball of right foot.

this on-line clubhead path is influenced largely by the alignment of your body—especially your shoulders—at address. Your alignment also helps determine how freely you can swing your arms and the club.

The proper alignment for you depends on your ability to create motion and free swinging. The so-called "square" alignment is best for most golfers. This alignment is such that lines across your shoulders, hips and knees would parallel the line from the ball to your intermediate target. The square alignment allows most players sufficient freedom of movement and gives them their best chance to swing the clubhead on the target line through impact.

Many golfers, unfortunately, set up with their shoulders aligned more "open" than the rest of the body. Right-handers align them too far to the left; left-handers to the right. Playing from an open shoulder position can create too much arm and shoulder tension that stifles freedom of arm movement and shoulder turning during the backswing. This tension later causes the right arm and shoulder to dominate the forward swing with a shoving or pushing movement. The legs cannot lead. The clubhead cuts across the ball from outside to inside the target line rather than along it.

The opposite extreme is the so-called "closed" alignment in which lines across the shoulders, hips and knees, if extended, would intersect the target line in front of the ball. Because this closed address position does allow a freer swinging and turning during the backswing, I prefer it to the open position. The drawback of the closed position is that it can make you swing so far inside going back that you stifle free turning of the hips and forward sliding of the knees during the forward swing.

While I feel that square alignment provides the best of two worlds—freedom of movement and on-line clubhead path—I think that advanced players who already have freedom of movement in their swings can play from a slightly open position. Less-skilled players who lack motion can make an easier and freer backswing from a slightly closed shoulder alignment. I would not advise a closed stance or hip alignment, however, since this would tend to stifle leg action on the forward swing.

7. Set your head back with chin turned. I feel you should position your head back of the ball, about over your right knee. This sets each shoulder slightly behind its respective knee. It establishes at address the same shoulder-knee relationship—knees leading, shoulders following—that you need to maintain in your forward swing to allow an explosive release of centrifugal force at just the right time.

Also, I feel that all players should develop the habit of turning their chin away from the ball slightly toward their right shoulder just before beginning the backswing. Jack Nicklaus, for one, feels that this move is vital to his game. Bob Toski, John Jacobs and other progressive instructors stress it in their teaching. This move not only clears the chin out of the way to allow a freer backswing but, if it's maintained well into your downswing, helps restrain your shoulders from uncoiling prematurely before your legs have a chance to lead and pull. It also sets your eye line parallel to the path along which your clubhead should move during your forward swing. Thus it programs you optically to work the clubhead back to the ball from inside to along the target line.

How bad setups ruin swings

On these pages and the two that follow we see the results of incorrect setup positions. The 18-handicap golfer shown above tends to crouch and hunch forward (first photo). He also plays the ball too far back in his stance (second photo). These factors force him to swing his club up and down on too steep a path, a problem that is accentuated by his right-side throwing action which straightens this arm prematurely in his downswing. To avoid chopping into the ground he must stiffen his legs. This lifts the clubhead's path by impact. He'll top many shots and, perhaps, blame the problem on "looking up." If he does, he'll hunch forward even more at address and further compound his basic problem.

This 13-handicap golfer addresses the ball with his right side too high. His right hip should be considerably lower than his left with his head well back of his hands. From this position he could turn his hips instead of swaying them laterally to the right going back and left going forward as he does now. Playing the ball farther forward in his stance would help this player set up with a lower right side which would, in turn, give him square contact more consistently.

This 16-handicap golfer addresses the ball with too much weight on his left foot instead of on the inside of the ball of his right. The improper distribution causes him to shift even more weight onto his left side during his backswing. With most of his weight already on his forward foot, he has little left to shift and drive toward the target during his forward swing. In time this man could eliminate his "reverse pivot" and add considerable distance to his shots by first squaring up his alignment and then setting up with most of his weight on the inside of his right foot.

Setting up with too much weight on the heels, and the ball played too far from the feet can result in an extremely flat swing, as we see here. This 20-handicapper reaches an extremely closed clubface position at the top of his backswing. On his forward swing his weight shifts from his heels to his toes so that he falls forward. He swings across the ball on an outside-in path with the face closed. The shot pull-hooks to the left. He'd swing on a more upright plane if he'd set his weight on the balls of his feet at address and bend forward a bit more from his hips.

Bad ball position can cause a player to misalign his body at address. This 12-handicap golfer plays the ball too far forward, outside his left foot. This forces his shoulders and hips into an open position, aligned well left of target. The open alignment causes his arms to swing on a flat backswing plane, taking the club so far to the inside that he must rely on his shoulders to return it to the target line by impact. His forward swing would be less of a shoulder shove if he'd simply play the ball a few inches back in his stance. This would square his shoulders and allow him to swing his arms more up and less around during his backswing. He'd then be in position to pull the club back through the ball along, rather than across, the target line.

4.

SETTING THE ANGLE

In this chapter I'm going to discuss how and when to cock your wrists.

I refer to cocking the wrists as "setting the angle." This term should not frighten even those of you who struggled with high school geometry. Setting the angle is a simple concept, but vital to the success of every golf swing.

The sides of the "angle" are your left arm and the clubshaft itself. The angle occurs at the top of the wrist of your left hand, at the base of the thumb.

You'll see what I mean if you take a golf club in your left hand and hold it out in front of you at arm's length, with your thumb on top of the shaft and your wrist in the straight-line Square Position. Extend your arm fully at shoulder level so your arm and the clubshaft form a straight line parallel to the ground.

Using only the last three fingers of this hand, cock the clubshaft upward to a vertical position. Your wrist should wrinkle on top, at the base of your thumb. The back of the wrist should not cup inward. You have just set the angle I'm talking about. That's what this chapter is all about—how to properly set this angle in your golf swing, when to set it and why to set it.

I want to strongly emphasize that setting the angle, or cocking the wrists, is not a solitary movement. The wrists cock and uncock in conjunction with over-all body and arm movement. I make this point because too often pupils stress wrist cock to the exclusion of a full body coil and free arm swing. As you cock and uncock your wrists in your swing, be sure that you also SWING.

Why set an angle?

The answer to this question should be fairly obvious. Imagine trying to swing a golf club stiff-wristed. You wouldn't hit it very far. You wouldn't have any flailing action.

In golf we are SWINGING an implement —the club. I can't think of any action in everyday living in which we swing an implement without some bending of either the arm, wrist or both. Even when driving a nail you bend your wrist somewhat—you set an angle and then release it.

Setting and releasing the angle increases centrifugal force. The way you build and release centrifugal force as you swing determines to a large extent the amount of clubhead speed you can produce and effectively transmit to the ball during impact.

Whenever you swing something around you in a circle, you produce centrifugal force. This force is pulling outward from the center of the circle—from you, yourself. When the object you are swinging has a weight on the far end—the clubhead—this force is increased. The force is also increased by the speed at which the object is moving.

Since the actual weight of the clubhead is constant throughout the golf swing, the factor that determines how much centrifugal force is available to be transferred to the ball is the speed at which the clubhead is moving during impact. Of course, striking the ball squarely is important too. The squareness of impact determines what percentage of your AVAILABLE force actually gets transferred.

Your ability to produce a maximum force during impact and to transfer that force squarely to the ball is directly related to how you set and retain and release the angle as you swing.

Most golfers realize that they don't always strike the ball squarely. They do not actually transfer 100 per cent of the energy of the moving clubhead DIRECTLY to the ball. It's easy to tell when you've mis-hit the ball. When it is contacted off-center on the clubface, it stings your hands and feels heavy as it's struck.

It's more difficult to determine whether you've released your maximum centrifugal force—produced maximum clubhead speed—just prior to and during impact. And most of us do not most of the time. High-speed and stop-action photography have shown us time and again that even in the best golf swings the rate of clubhead acceleration, if not actual clubhead speed, begins to decline PRIOR to impact. Thus the job we all face is to preserve clubhead speed, to detain as long as possible the release of centrifugal force in our downswings.

In the next chapter I will tell you how to delay this release. But your ability to retain your angle depends largely on how you set it in the first place. Setting the angle improperly makes the job of retaining it until the right time all but impossible.

How to set your angle

Maintaining maximum clubhead speed and producing square contact during impact is best achieved with a swing that PULLS the club into position during the early stages of the forward swing. If you throw, shove or push it forward from the top of your backswing, centrifugal force is either wasted

Set your angle while swinging freely

"Setting the angle" describes the process of cocking the wrists. The Angle in question is that formed by the left arm and the clubshaft. Proper setting is done with the last three fingers of the left hand. The angle will be retained well into the downswing if these fingers continue to control the clubshaft, as they should in the Square-to-Square swing. Professional Dave Hill, shown here in the top photos, sets his angle earlier than most professionals. Readers will note, however, that his wrists still cock gradually throughout his backswing. Angle setting should not be an independent movement. It should be combined with a free swinging of the arms and a full turning of the body, as evidenced here in Hill's swing.

Early setting can lead to mere lifting of the club if not combined with this freedom of movement. The 18-handicap golfer in the bottom photos also sets his angle early, but fails to combine his wrist cocking with a free arm swing. He lifts the club up and pulls his right elbow away from his side. This puts him into position to throw, rather than pull, the club on his forward swing. A premature loss of angle—and clubhead speed—results.

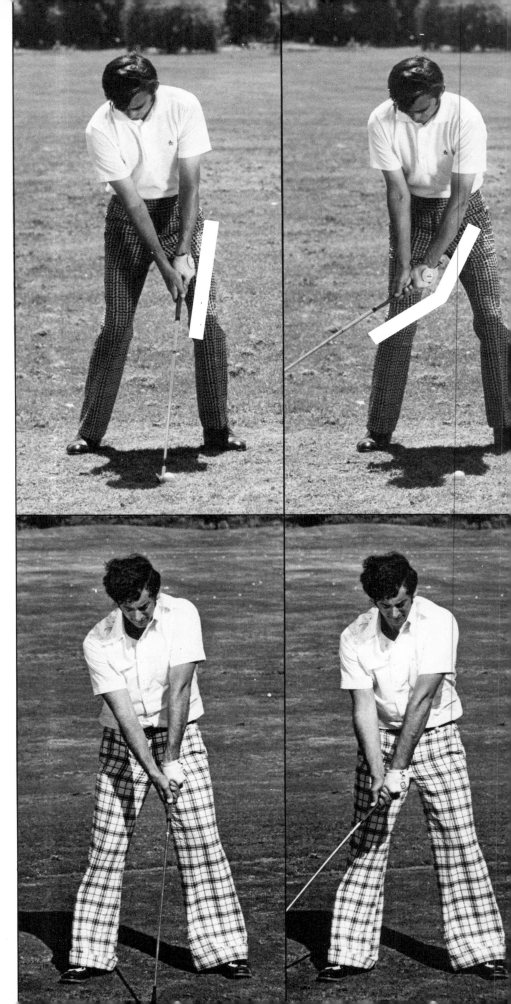

prematurely or never fully released, or the swing path is altered so the clubhead doesn't strike the ball squarely.

As I described in Chapter One, pulling the club early in your forward swing requires active use of muscles that normally play a subordinate role in most of the things we do in everyday living. Throwing and shoving employ muscles that normally play a dominant role. Therefore the pulling action on the forward swing is largely a skill that we must learn.

To set the stage for pulling the club on the forward swing, you must learn to set the angle in a way that (1) breaks down the influence of normally dominant muscles and (2) builds up the role of normally subordinate muscles.

Specifically, you should seek to set the angle—to cock your wrists—with the last three fingers of your left hand. When these fingers assume control, they activate the muscles on the underside of your left forearm. It is these three fingers and these under-forearm muscles, along with your legs, that should lead and pull the clubshaft into position during your forward swing. So long as these muscles control the clubshaft you can pull the club forward, delay your release of centrifugal force and also maintain on-line movement of the clubhead longer through the impact area.

Most golfers do not control the club with these fingers. The normal tendency is to

throw the club forward with the right hand, the hand that is behind the clubshaft when it's moving forward. The normal tendency is also to shove the club forward with the right shoulder. Whenever these normally dominant parts take over, we lose the angle we set on our backswing too early in our forward swing. We dissipate centrifugal force long before the clubhead meets the ball. Also, we throw or shove the clubhead across, rather than along, the target line. We waste clubhead speed and reduce our chances for square striking—we lose both accuracy and distance.

The act of setting the angle properly with the last three fingers of the left hand begins with how you hold the club. As I've mentioned, you should grip the shaft with just enough pressure in these three fingers to establish a sensitivity that they are going to play the lead role in setting the angle. The tighter you grip with the thumb and forefinger of your right hand, the more difficult it becomes for these last three fingers to play this dominant role.

You should reinforce this sensitivity by the way you waggle the club prior to starting your actual swing. Your waggle should preview your takeaway. You should waggle the clubhead two feet or more away from and back to the ball with these last three fingers doing the work. You should feel that these three fingers are forcing your right hand to submit. The last three fingers of your left hand should feel alert and active; your right hand, wrist and arm should feel soft and passive, ready to fold during your backswing. (See page 122 for specific drill on how to waggle.)

Most good golfers waggle the same way every time. They take three waggles every time, or four waggles every time, or six or seven. A consistent waggle breeds consistent grip pressure from shot to shot.

The actual setting of the angle during the backswing should be done smoothly and with these last three fingers. Avoid sudden squeezing; avoid jerking. Avoid producing any excessive tension that might restrict your freedom of motion. Your goal is to cock your wrists while establishing just enough control with these three fingers so that you can maintain it throughout your backswing and forward swing.

As you cock your wrists—set your angle—with these last three fingers, you should move into the Square Position. Once in this position, the back of your left hand, wrist and forearm form a straight-line relationship. You should see no inward cupping or outward bowing at the back of this wrist. The only bending of your left wrist is at the base of your thumb, not at the back of the wrist.

It is extremely important that your clubface does not close or hood as you move into this straight-line Square Position during your takeaway. In previous writings on the Square-to-Square Method, the first step in cocking the wrists was called "curling under."

This referred to a gentle inward squeezing with the last three fingers of the left hand. "Curling under" is a phrase that I helped coin. It was designed to establish left-hand control, break down right hand-wrist-arm tension and put the golfer in the Square Position.

Unfortunately, anything in golf can be overdone. Many readers interpreted "curling under" to mean such an extreme counter-clockwise turning of the hands that the right wrist actually began to crawl over the left during the takeaway and lock. This produced an extreme closing of the clubface and forced the right elbow to wing out from the player's side. The right-arm tension that curling under intended to reduce, actually increased. This increased tension cut off backswings and caused shoving and pushing on downswings. For many players, curling under produced a contrived takeaway that inhibited freedom of motion.

My experience in recent years has been that the phrase "setting the angle" and the technique it encompasses avoids these pitfalls and makes it easier to move into the Square Position. Setting the angle causes the right wrist to fold back and the right elbow to move inward toward your side and allows the tension-free backswing needed to put the shaft in position from where it can, in fact, be pulled.

Setting the angle with the last three fingers of your left hand will tend to make you swing

Establish left-hand control

Correct setting of the angle requires control of the clubshaft largely with the last three fingers of the left hand—the "pulling hand"—in the backswing. When combined with a light right-hand grip pressure, this left-hand control breaks down tension in the right wrist, elbow and shoulder area during the backswing. With the right side thus decontrolled, the golfer will be less likely to throw, push or shove with it during his forward swing. The photos of Bobby Nichols in the top row show the left hand-arm control that forces his right wrist and elbow to fold gently during his backswing. He can thus retain his angle deep into the forward swing. The photos of a 13-handicap amateur in the bottom row show how right-arm tension early in the backswing prohibits the wrists from cocking until near the top. This late setting of the angle causes the player to flip the rebounding clubshaft from the top with his right hand and arm. He loses his wrist cock prematurely, long before impact, and thus wastes clubhead speed.

your arms on a proper plane instead of one that is too flat. Swinging back too flat forces you to throw or shove the clubhead with your right side in your downswing in order to get it back to the target line. A proper plane on your backswing will allow you to pull your club back to the line. This will allow you to keep your clubhead moving along the target line for a longer span through the impact area, so long as your legs lead your shoulders in your downswing and you continue to control the club with the last three fingers of your left hand. The result will be more shots that start toward your target.

You will find it easier to set the angle correctly if you hold the club lightly with your right hand. The tighter you grip with this hand, the more left-hand control you'll need to break down tension in your right arm and shoulder area.

Again, anything in golf can be overdone, even the amount of control you establish in the last three fingers of your left hand. It is possible to squeeze these fingers too tightly and produce too much tension in your left arm and shoulder. This tension decreases your ability to swing the club smoothly.

You will also find it easier to set your angle correctly if your swing tempo is relatively slow, rather than fast. Most golfers have a built-in swing tempo, or swing pace. We all swing to our own particular "beat." Any departure from your normal tempo is likely to hinder, if not ruin, the rhythm and timing of your over-all swing. Swinging back and up faster than normal almost surely will cause you to lose some control of the club. In trying to regain this lost control later in your swing, you almost surely will do so with your dominant right hand—your throwing hand.

While it is easier to set and maintain left-hand control if you have a relatively slow swing pace, you should not try to slow your normal backswing tempo too much. Subconsciously you'll sense that you're not going to hit the ball very far. This also creates undue right-side pressure on your forward swing as you try to re-establish a more forceful swing. You will tend to grab and throw the club with your right hand or shove it forward with your right arm and shoulder.

We are simply trying to set the angle in a way that it can be readily retained until late in the downswing with left-hand control. If your left hand isn't in control during your backswing, it certainly will not be in control during your forward swing.

Keep moving

I want to stress the need for maintaining motion as you set the angle and swing. Any time you try to incorporate something new into your swing, especially when it involves a change in your backswing, you risk reducing your freedom of movement. You tend to lose your sense of rhythm for a while.

The mere act of concentrating on something new creates a certain amount of mental tension. This mental tension inhibits freedom of movement. Your swing tends to become a mechanical act, rather than a swing.

Therefore, let me clarify the need for blending arm swinging and body turning with setting the angle. I think my friend and fellow teacher, Bob Toski, describes the golf swing beautifully. Bob points out that during the backswing the arms must swing freely so that the shoulders tilt and turn AS A RESULT. The swinging arms should turn the shoulders, rather than the turning shoulders swing the arms. If you cannot sense that your shoulder turn is a result of your free arm swing, then your arms are too tense.

Concentrating on setting the angle properly can also stifle freedom of body motion. Therefore we need some rule of thumb on how much the hips should turn during the backswing. I personally feel that you should let your legs and hips turn and coil as much as seems comfortable—*so long as your right knee remains flexed throughout your backswing.* This means that if your arms swing freely your hips can turn as much as you want, so long as you never shift your weight to the OUTSIDE of the heel of your right foot.

When to set your angle

Setting the angle is a gradual process. It should be done smoothly, without jerking the clubhead upward quickly. Still, though the process is gradual, some golfers do most of their angle setting earlier than others. There are advantages and disadvantages in both early setting and late setting. I'll mention these so that you can determine for yourself whether you should be an early-setter or a late-setter. While you must set your angle gradually, for descriptive purposes I'll categorize golfers into three types, according to when they do the MAJORITY of their angle setting. These categories are (1) swing and set, (2) swinging set and (3) set and swing.

Swing and Set describes a relatively late setting of the angle. The wrists are largely cocked near or at the top of the backswing and in some cases further cocked early in the forward swing. Frequently the hands and hips lead the clubhead away from the ball during the takeaway. Examples of swing-and-setters are Jack Nicklaus, Bruce Crampton and, during his competitive days, Byron Nelson.

Generally speaking, late setting is best for players whose swings are relatively inhibited, who need more body turn. Late setting allows such turning because the body turns almost fully before the wrists do much of their cocking.

While late setting does allow the free turning that we all need to make a rhythmical swing, only outstanding athletes—like Nicklaus and Crampton—can set the angle so late and still exert a sufficient pulling

Swing freely, turn freely

It is important to turn freely while setting the angle during the backswing. The hips and shoulders should be allowed to turn fully as a result of the arms swinging the club, so long as the right leg remains flexed at the knee, as shown in the photo of Sam Snead on the facing page. The amateur at top-left has turned his hips so much that his leg has stiffened. He will have difficulty leading with his legs on his forward swing. Instead he will tend to throw and shove the club back to the target line with his right side. The amateur at bottom-left has retained his right-leg flex but has not turned fully, largely because he's lifted the club instead of having swung it freely with his arms.

Ready to pull

In the past, leading golfers such as Tommy Armour and Bobby Locke (top and bottom photos shown above) allowed the back of the left wrist to cup inward at the top of the backswing. This generally put the clubface into an "open" position that would cause slicing unless they could square it to the line by impact with a strong right-handed throw on the forward swing. No wonder Armour, for one, advocated full use of the right hand on the downswing. Most modern professionals set their angle with maximum control centered in the last three fingers of their left hand. This control sets the back of the left hand, wrist and lower forearm in the straight-line Square Position, ideal for pulling with the left hand and arm in the downswing. Since the clubface is already in a square position at the top of the swing, no right-hand manipulation is needed to square it by impact. The modern pros grouped around Gary Player are—clockwise from top-left—Susie Berning, Kathy Whitworth, Dale Hayes and Tom Weiskopf. Readers who lack sufficient left-hand control to establish and maintain the ideal straight-line Square Position are urged to follow the drills that appear in Chapter 7.

force on the clubshaft during the forward swing. Cocking the wrists so late in the swing, when the club is traveling at a relatively fast speed, often causes a wristiness and a flipping of the clubhead at the top of the swing. The left wrist collapses out of the straight-line Square Position and cups inward. The club then "rebounds" into the downswing with the right hand taking over and throwing it through the impact area. Clubhead speed is wasted and the clubhead moves off the target line and upward too soon. Topped shots often result.

Golfers who set the angle late need strong left-hand control and strong legwork on their forward swing to maintain a pulling action into the downswing. Nicklaus and Crampton have it. Nelson had it. Most golfers, especially women, do not.

Late setting also requires a relatively slow backswing and a slow start into the forward swing— a la Nicklaus—to minimize the rebounding effect and the right-hand takeover.

Because late setting does not establish left-hand control early in the backswing, the right arm often remains too tense. The right elbow may wing out too far away from the body. This puts the club into position to be shoved forward, rather than pulled.

To summarize, the swing-and-set technique is valid if not vital for golfers who need more body turn or motion in their backswings —most beginners, for instance. However, to advance to a high level in the game using this technique calls for excellent rhythm and timing, a relatively slow swing pace, strong left-hand control and outstanding lower body and leg leadership on the forward swing. Such fine tuning demands a great deal of constant practice.

The Swinging Set: This technique finds the wrists hinging gradually during the backswing—from start to finish—with little or no additional cocking early in the forward swing. Many good players now use the swinging set. Among the pros these include Arnold Palmer, Bert Yancey, Sam Snead, Tommy Bolt, Ben Hogan and Frank Beard.

The swinging set does not encourage quite so much freedom of movement as the swing-and-set style, but it does provide a somewhat earlier establishment of left-hand dominance. There is less likelihood of losing control of the club at the top of the swing and then grabbing hold with the right hand. Golfers who combine the swinging set with strong left-hand control and good leg action on the forward swing—like Bolt—can swing at a relatively faster pace and still pull, instead of throw, the club forward to the ball.

Set and Swing: Here the angle is set largely before the hands reach shoulder height during the backswing. Control of the club is maintained in the last three fingers of the left hand throughout the entire swing. Generally the clubhead leads the hands, arms and hips away from the ball. The golfer moves into the straight-line Square Position during his takeaway. This puts him into ideal position for square impact from the start. No further manipulation of the clubshaft with the hands is necessary; centrifugal force will uncock the wrists and square the clubface just prior to impact.

The set-and-swing technique not only establishes left-hand, left-side control early, but in so doing places the club in excellent position to be pulled—not thrown or shoved—during the forward swing. This technique often produces a relatively upright arm swing. It all but eliminates flippiness at the top of the backswing.

The late Tony Lema was an excellent example of a set-and-swing golfer. Current stars who set the angle relatively early include Lee Trevino, Johnny Miller, Tom Weiskopf, Dave Hill, Lanny Wadkins and Grier Jones.

An early setting of the angle is best suited to golfers who already have long, free-flowing swings with plenty of body turn. It is the best method for developing the target-side dominance you need to increase clubhead speed and on-line movement of the clubhead through impact.

The set-and-swing golfer must take care that he sets the angle while his arms swing freely and thus turn his shoulders and hips fully. Early setting does encourage picking up the club with the hands and arms in a jerky, rhythm-inhibiting movement during the takeaway.

Thus, while the set-and-swing technique is ideal for playing Square-to Square because it breaks down right-arm tension and minimizes our normal inclination to throw, shove or push the club back to the ball, it can reduce freedom of movement. It can make you swing like a totem pole with arms. Therefore, do not try the early wrist cock until you have first developed a free and full arm swing and a full hip turn, both away from and back to the target.

When setting the angle early there also may be a tendency to feel that you have already completed your shoulder turn before you really have, and are ready to swing back to the ball before you really are. I suggest that in learning to set the angle early you first make a conscious effort to make a slow, full arm swing going back, letting the swinging of your arms pull your left shoulder down and around as far as it will comfortably go.

Let me stress once again that freedom of movement is the key to any type of golf swing. Please do not let your attention to setting your angle deter you from swinging freely with a relatively light grip pressure.

3 great players set and retain angle

On this page and the 23 that follow, we'll compare the swings of Tom Weiskopf, Arnold Palmer and Jack Nicklaus from both the "face-on" and "down-the-line" vantage points. Readers will note the slight, but vital, differences in the timing of when each sets his angle. Weiskopf is considered a member of the early-setting "set and swing" school. Palmer, with a "swinging set," cocks his wrists later. Nicklaus sets his angle latest of all and definitely fits the "swing and set" category. Again, the angle is that formed by the clubshaft and the left arm.

2 feet back

Though their clubheads have moved only about two feet away from the ball, all the players, even the relatively late-setting Nicklaus, have begun to set the angle. Note that Weiskopf and Palmer have moved the clubhead from ahead of to behind their hands. Nicklaus has moved from the straight club-arm relationship into a slight, but definite, wrist cock. All three players show a slight folding at the back of the right wrist, which had been straight in the preceding photos. This folding indicates that the angle is being set with the last three fingers of the left hand in each case.

Left hand belt high

With their left hands near belt-buckle height, we begin to see the results that occur from proper setting of the angle. The down-the-line photos, especially, show Weiskopf with right-side submissiveness—more hinging of the right wrist and folding of the right elbow—than Palmer and Nicklaus, a result of his relatively early wrist cock. Palmer shows more than the late-setting Nicklaus, but all show definite left hand-arm dominance and club control. Note also that all three have moved into the straight-line Square Position at the back of their left wrist by this stage in their backswings.

Left arm horizontal

With the left arm now parallel to the ground in each case, we can clearly distinguish the variation in the degree of angle set thus far by each player. The reader will note that Weiskopf's clubshaft is almost vertical. Palmer, with less wrist cock to this point, has yet to reach this shaft position but still has cocked his wrists more than Nicklaus. Most of Jack's angle setting will come later, even during his downswing. A result of his late setting is seen here in the fact that his right elbow is starting to fly up and away from his side. Earlier setting would help fold it into his side.

Hips turned fullest amount

In these photos we see each player at the stage of his swing at which his hips and legs have turned their fullest. They are ready to reverse direction. A comparison of the club's position in these photos with those on the next two pages shows it continues moving back while the player's left knee starts its downswing movement. Golfers who swing back too fast and/or with too little left-hand control will either lose their grip on the club at this point or turn over dominance to their throwing hand.

Clubshaft swung fullest amount

Here we see photos taken when the club's shaft has reached its apex and is ready to start back to the ball. Note that it's moved beyond where it appeared in the preceding photos while the left knee has already started gliding toward the ball (lines indicate players' previous knee positions). This move initiates the pulling action that is the crux of the Square-to-Square Method. A slow-moving and passive right hand and arm at this point is vital for maintaining left-hand control and retaining the angle. Late-setters such as Nicklaus need exceptional right-hand passiveness and slow arm pace to avoid a rebounding of the clubshaft from the top or grabbing with the throwing hand.

Pulling forward from below

These photos best illustrate how leading with the legs helps the left hand and arm exert a pulling, rather than a throwing, force on the clubshaft. Note that each player's left knee already has slid closer to the target than any part of the upper body. The shoulders are still largely coiled, playing their proper role as followers. Each player has retained all of his angle, if not actually increased it. This would not be the case had the right hand taken over from the top of the swing.

Hands hip high

Only at this point, with the hands near hip height on the downswing, do we see these players first starting to release some of their wrist cock. This loss of angle occurs solely as a result of centrifugal force pulling outward along the clubshaft. It would have happened sooner if these players were not controlling the clubshaft with the last three fingers of their pulling hands. They would have wasted clubhead speed prematurely, as happens to amateur golfers who feel that right-hand throwing of the clubhead will add length to the shot.

Near impact

At this point there is nothing the golfer can do to improve the shot, but a great deal to ruin it. Specifically, he can grab the clubshaft—perhaps anticipating contact with the ball. This rapid increase of grip pressure will tighten the wrists and arms and prevent a free rotation of the club. The club will remain slightly open at impact and the ball will slice left to right. Or the player may quit accelerating his arms and throw the clubhead with his hands into a closed, hooking position. Proper releasing of the angle demands a free arm acceleration through impact—as these players surely demonstrate—with no grabbing of the clubshaft.

Through the ball

All three of these players are still releasing their angle during impact. This fact is indicated by the slight bend still present at the back of the right hand, except in the photo of Weiskopf taken slightly after contact. All three have retained some left-knee flex, indicating good leg action earlier. Palmer has less than the others because of his slightly wider stance and inside swing path. All three strike the ball with the back of the left hand, wrist and lower forearm still in the straight-line Square Position, an indication of clubshaft command with the last three fingers of this hand.

Following through

All three players continue to rotate the club freely during the follow-through with no breaking down or inward cupping at the back of the left wrist. At this point all three players are still in the Square Position. Both arms are more or less extended and relatively close together, indicating a free swinging of the arms through the ball and beyond. This free swinging not only serves to square the clubface by impact, but also keeps the clubhead moving down the line and at ball level for a relatively long span.

At the finish

These finish positions clearly show the result of pulling force in the forward swing. In the photos below note how each player's hands have swung well above and to the left of his head indicating free swinging of the arms on a proper plane. In the face-on photos note the weight has shifted fully onto the outside of the left foot and the left knee is still flexed, a result of legs leading shoulders on the downswing. Each player's hips have turned through to face the target and each finishes high on his right toe.

5.
RETAINING THE ANGLE

Everything I've said up to now has been designed to accomplish one goal: to put you, the golfer, into position and into a state of muscular readiness to PULL the club from the top of the swing back through the impact area.

I've told you how to hold the club in a way that gives you your best chance to pull it down and forward with the last three fingers of your left hand—your pulling hand—in control.

I've told you how to set up to the ball so that your legs—especially your left knee—will aid you in this pulling effort, working actively as leaders rather than passively as followers in your forward swing.

I've explained how to break down tension in your right hand, your right arm and your shoulders because it is tension in these areas that inhibits pulling and, instead, promotes shoving and pushing.

I've attempted to break down this tension by suggesting a constantly light grip with your right hand, a soft right arm and, above all, a free swinging of your arms.

I've asked you to waggle and to set your angle—cock your wrists—with the last three fingers of your left hand, again to establish left-hand control to pull the club forward and to break down tension in your right wrist and arm.

Finally, I've described the Square Position wherein the back of your left hand, wrist and forearm form a straight-line relationship. This is the position that best allows you to pull the club downward and forward with sufficient left-hand and target-side control. I've asked you to either assume the Square Position at address or early in your backswing, and to retain it as long as possible during your forward swing. In short, I've asked you to swing Square-to-Square.

This chapter is about retaining the angle that you set between your left arm and the clubshaft during your backswing. This is the angle you set when you cock your left wrist at the base of the thumb.

Angle set, angle retained

Having cocked his wrists—set the angle—relatively early in his backswing (top photo), Tommy Bolt retains this angle well into his downswing (bottom photo). Thus he withholds the release of centrifugal force—clubhead speed—until near impact and puts himself in position to swing the clubhead down the line. Retaining the angle this deep into the downswing requires that his legs, left arm and left hand pull the club into position while his shoulders and right arm and hand remain relatively passive. Maintaining the Square Position helps Bolt control the clubshaft largely with the last three fingers of his left hand.

Your goal from this point on is to retain this wrist cock as late into your downswing as possible, but not so long that it never gets fully released by impact. The longer you can retain your wrist cock, yet fully release it during impact, the more centrifugal force you will transfer to the ball in the form of additional clubhead speed.

To achieve a full release you must hold the club lightly and swing your arms freely throughout your forward swing. This free-swinging release not only produces a full explosion of centrifugal force, but also helps to (1) square the clubface to the target line, (2) swing it along that line and (3) extend the left arm and clubshaft to put the clubface at ball level—all during impact.

Our method for retaining the angle is, again, to apply largely a pulling force rather than a throwing, shoving or pushing force. The more you pull the club with your left side, the longer you retain your angle. The more you throw the club with your right hand, the sooner you tend to lose your angle and dissipate clubhead speed prematurely. The more you shove or push the club forward with your right arm or shoulder, the more you inhibit your ability to pull and minimize your chances of making square contact with the clubhead moving along the flight path.

To pull any object, a large part of you must be in front of it. To throw an object, a large part of you must be behind it. In golf the

Retaining the angle

Bruce Crampton's strong driving results largely from his ability to retain the angle formed by his left arm and clubshaft until late in his downswing, yet still release this wrist cock fully by impact. His clubhead accelerates into the ball. Too much right-hand grip pressure during his downswing would force his wrists to uncock sooner and waste clubhead speed too early. Excessive arm and shoulder tension would delay the uncocking too long and prohibit squaring of the clubface. His shot would slice to the right.

Losing the angle

Too much right-hand grip pressure causes this 12-handicap player to lose his wrist cock much earlier than does Crampton. He expends centrifugal force too soon. By the time his clubhead reaches the ball, it is decelerating. He doesn't drive the ball as far as he could if he had maintained left-hand control and a light, passive hold on the club with his right hand. This player's tendency to pressure the clubshaft with his right hand results largely from his exceedingly short and flat backswing that puts him into a position from which he must throw and shove, rather than pull, the clubhead back to the target line.

object you pull or throw is the clubshaft. Since your left hand is in front of the clubshaft —on the target side—as you swing back to the ball, this is your pulling hand. Your right hand, because it's behind the clubshaft, is your throwing hand. Thus, to pull your golf club into position—to best retain your angle —your left hand must control the clubshaft early in your downswing. More specifically, the last three fingers of this hand must retain the control you instilled in them as you gripped the club, waggled it at address and set your angle during your backswing.

For your pulling hand to control your downswing, it is best to retain a light, passive grip with your throwing hand. For most golfers this requires conscious effort. Our instinct is to rely on this normally dominant hand as a source of power. The farther we try to strike the ball the more we tend to increase grip pressure in our throwing hand.

The best way I know to retain control with your pulling hand is to maintain your Square Position through impact and on to the finish of your swing. This will allow you to move through impact with your left hand leading the clubhead itself slightly. Excessive pressuring of the clubshaft with your throwing hand will break down the straight-line relationship at the back of your left wrist and force your clubhead to lead, rather than follow, this hand through impact.

Again, however, let me caution that too much grip pressure with even the left hand can also inhibit a free release and a free swinging of the arms.

In all good golfers we see that while the back of the left wrist remains firm and uncupped throughout most of the forward swing, it does rotate counterclockwise a full 180 degrees. This rotation occurs as the arms swing from one side of the body to the other. The back of the left hand, wrist and lower forearm turn a half circle, just as if they were a page turning in this book. Without this free rotation you cannot square your clubface back to the target during impact except by flipping it with your right hand or shoving it with your right shoulder. Players who find their clubface opens to the right of target at impact will, for a time, need to consciously develop this rotation. They will need work on turning the grip end of the club with the last three fingers of the left hand and left forearm during their forward swings. Those developing this movement should seek the feeling that the back of the left hand is turning and facing downward just past impact. If you try this and hook violently to the left, you are forcing this rotation with your throwing hand, as opposed to producing it with the last three fingers of your pulling hand. At the end of this book I have included a drill to produce this rotation and to strengthen the underside muscles of the left forearm that produce it.

Another way to retain left-hand control is

Ready to pull

To retain the angle well into one's downswing, the normally weaker left arm and hand must assume a dominant role. They must pull the clubshaft down and forward and offset the normal tendency to throw and shove with the stronger shoulders and right arm and hand. To aid in this pulling effort, the left knee must lead the forward swing. This photo of Lee Trevino dramatically shows the pulling action he achieves by sliding this knee toward the target. Note how his shoulders have remained relatively coiled while his right arm stays passively folded.

Shoulders
still coiled

Right arm soft,
passive,
still folded

Left knee leads

Legs lead, shoulders follow

Further evidence that the legs should lead the down-swing is shown in the photos on this page of (top to bottom) Gene Littler, Jack Nicklaus and Lanny Wadkins. Note in the right-hand photo of each set that each player's knees have already returned to about the same alignment they were in at address (left-hand photos) while his shoulders are still relatively coiled. As a result each retains the angle and swings his clubhead from inside to along the target line, reaching maximum speed at impact.

92

Legs lag, shoulders uncoil

In comparison with the professionals on the facing page, the amateur on this page fails to lead with his legs on the forward swing. By the time his knees have returned to the alignment they were in at address, his shoulders have uncoiled almost fully. They are "top-heavy" in their forward swings. As a result he is unable to retain the angle. He wastes centrifugal force prior to impact and tends to shove the clubhead into the ball from outside the target line. Rushing one's downswing in a misguided effort to hit the ball far is a major cause of top-heaviness.

to start your downswing at a leisurely pace. The faster your hands move the club from the top of your swing, the sooner your throwing hand will take over and dissipate your angle. Here is why this happens:

At the top of your backswing your hands must change direction from a back and upward flow of motion to a down and forward flow. You must give yourself time to make this switch in direction. If you quickly move your hands down and forward while your club is still swinging back and up, the weight of the moving clubhead will begin to tear the shaft loose in your hands. To regain your hold on the club you will subconsciously grab it with your dominant right hand. This rapid increase in right-hand grip pressure will force you to THROW the clubhead back toward the ball. You will lose your angle—and clubhead speed—prematurely. You will "hit from the top."

I suggest you liken the changing of direction at the top of your backswing to turning a sharp corner in your automobile. You should resist the temptation to accelerate your hands, arms and shoulders down and forward just as you resist a sudden uncontrolled acceleration of your car while turning the corner.

Your throwing hand is always battling your pulling hand for control of the club early in the downswing. Hopefully your pulling hand will win the fight, but not by strangling the clubshaft to the point that you cannot swing your arms and rotate the club freely. If your left hand does maintain control by pulling, it will remain firm and dominant over your right arm—your throwing arm—through impact.

In the war between your pulling hand and throwing hand, each has a major ally. Your pulling hand and arm are supported in the battle by your legs. Your throwing hand and arm are closely allied with your shoulders.

The more time you allow yourself to change directions at the top of your swing, the more time you give your feet and legs to lead your forward swing and help you pull the clubshaft toward impact.

I feel that the first move you should make in your downswing is to glide your left knee forward and outward toward your left toe. We see indication of this in the swings of good players. The space between their knees widens early in their downswing (see picture of Lee Trevino on page 91). The widening will not occur if you "push off" from the inside of your right foot as some golf instruction has heretofore suggested. I believe that pushing off the right foot may help put the legs into a role of active leadership in the forward swing, but too often it causes the left leg and side to stiffen and stop. When you stiffen and stop your pulling side, all that you can do thereafter is throw the clubhead forward with your right hand and hook the ball violently, or push and

shove it forward with your right arm and shoulder and pull, pull-slice or slice the shot.

I feel that the left knee should first glide toward your left toe and then gradually rotate laterally back to the left of target as the hips uncoil. It should remain flexed until after you have struck the ball.

There are two major problems that all golfers encounter sooner or later. One is releasing the angle too soon—hitting from the top—and wasting centrifugal force. The other is "coming over the top," which occurs when your right shoulder, instead of your left knee, starts your downswing. This shoulder swings out and around instead of down and under. It forces your right elbow away from, rather than into, your side. Your clubhead eventually swings out beyond your target line before reaching the ball. By impact it is cutting back to the inside. It cuts ACROSS the ball instead of moving down the line and squarely into the back of it.

Releasing too soon and coming over the top occur when your right hand and shoulder, respectively, win the battle for downswing supremacy. Leading with your left knee and pacing the swing with your left arm can offset the instinct to over-control the clubshaft with your shoulders and your throwing hand.

You'll hit your shots farther and straighter much more consistently if your swing follows the pattern I mentioned earlier. On the backswing your arms should swing freely and your shoulders coil automatically AS A RESULT. On the forward swing your legs should lead and fling your arms. Your shoulders should uncoil automatically. Remember: arms coil shoulders; legs fling arms. That's the concept involved, but to put it into effect you should try to develop the feeling that on BOTH backswing and forward swing your shoulders coil and uncoil passively AS A RESULT of your arms swinging freely. Ideally, the shoulders are always followers.

A free arm swing is very important. When your arms swing freely your swing has the grace, flow and motion that we sense in the swings of the touring pros. Your swing needs motion to be rhythmical. Given proper

Old master, modern swing

Byron Nelson, winner of 45 PGA tournaments, dominated the pro tour in the early- to mid-1940's with a swing that was one of the first to employ several modern Square-to-Square techniques. Note how Nelson pulls the club during his downswing with his legs leading and his knees flexed throughout, and with his left hand, wrist and forearm in the Square Position. Thus he retained the angle longer and moved his clubhead down the line farther through the impact area than did most of his contemporaries.

Legs fling the arms

To pull an object, something must be in front of it
leading the way. In the modern golf swing, the left knee
is the leader in the forward swing. It remains flexed
throughout and helps the player's arms fling forward
with the club trailing behind, seemingly never to
catch up. On the opposite page are three excellent
examples of the legs flinging the arms during the forward
swings of (from top to bottom) Tommy Bolt, the late
Tony Lema and Jerry Heard. Note how their left knees
all slide toward the target and then swivel around to
the left as the hips turn out of the way. Maintaining
knee flex as they do keeps the clubhead moving at ball
level for a longer span. On this page we see a good
amateur golfer who occasionally pushes shots to the
right or hooks to the left because his legs stiffen and
his hips fail to turn through freely.

Left-side control through impact

Modern professionals such as Jim Colbert (opposite page) and Bobby Nichols, Ben Crenshaw and Arnold Palmer (top to bottom at left) make solid contact consistently because they extend the duration in which their clubhead moves along the target line at ball level. They increase this span of on-line movement by retaining firm left-side control through impact. This control is evidenced by their retention of the Square Position in which the back of the left hand, wrist and forearm remain in a firm straight-line relationship. The amateur golfer shown above loses this position because of excessive right-side pressure—throwing and shoving —on the back of the clubshaft earlier in his forward swing. Note how his left wrist cups inward and his clubhead lifts abruptly as a result.

Release the angle freely to square the clubface

Maximum distance and accuracy require not only retaining the angle deep into the downswing, but also releasing it—uncocking the wrists—freely. Releasing freely returns the clubhead to ball level and allows the arms to rotate the clubface back to an on-target alignment by the time it reaches impact. Thereafter the arms continue to turn the clubface freely as it swings back to inside the target line. A free releasing of the angle depends on a free turning of the hips and a free swinging of the arms, as opposed to shoving with the shoulders. Here we see J. C. Snead releasing freely while maintaining sufficient left-hand control to retain the straight-line Square Position throughout.

posture and body alignment at address, if your arms swing freely going back, your body will coil fully for a maximum build-up of power. If your arms swing freely on your forward swing, following the gliding action of your left knee, you will release this power fully into the ball.

Tension, both physical and mental, stifles motion. Too much grip pressure (physical tension) in either hand tightens your arms and impedes their free movement. Mental tensions, such as fear of not striking the ball squarely or misdirecting it into trouble or trying to hit it an extra few yards, cause you to over-control the club, to guide or steer or force it back to the ball. This over-control creates undue hand and arm tension that stifles free swinging and consistency of movement. In the final chapter I will deal with mental tensions and how to overcome them. Also in that chapter I suggest certain drills and playing techniques to help you set and retain the angle and maintain your Square Position in a pulling swing.

For the moment, however, here is a summary of ways to help you better retain your angle deeper into your forward swing. Pick the two or three thoughts you feel will be most helpful.

—Hold the club very lightly as you swing your arms freely to the top of your backswing.

—Start your forward swing by gliding your flexed left knee toward your left toe.

—Sense control of the club with the last three fingers of your left hand throughout your swing, especially as you pull early in your forward swing.

—Maintain a slight pressure between the left thumb and the heel pad of the right hand at the top of your backswing.

—Keep your right hand and arm light and passive as you start your forward swing.

—Swing your arms as slowly at the start of your forward swing as you did at the start of your backswing.

—Sense that your legs are pulling or flinging your arms forward.

—Sense that your clubhead will move into the ball from slightly inside the target line.

—Sense that your clubhead is not going to pass your hands until after impact.

—Accelerate your left arm through— not just to—impact.

—Rotate the clubshaft counterclockwise through impact with the last three fingers of your left hand while maintaining your Square Position.

Free arm swing squares clubface

Sam Snead (bottom-left) swings his arms freely and lets his shoulders FOLLOW as a result. His free-swinging arms turn the clubface back to square at impact, with the back of his left hand, wrist and forearm remaining firmly in the Square Position throughout. Conversely, the 36-handicap golfer (top-left) SHOVES his arms forward with his shoulders. This slows his arm speed so much that he cannot freely square the clubface by impact, even though his clubhead is moving much slower than Snead's. Instead he must rely on his right hand to throw the clubhead back to square. Although he appears to make fairly good contact, he will not do so consistently because this right-hand throw breaks down his left wrist—note the inward cupping—which will move his clubhead upward and off the target line too abruptly.

6.
FINISH LIKE A PRO

The purpose of this chapter is to help you build an understanding and a heightened awareness or feel of what is really happening in your particular golf swing. I'm going to tell you how to analyze yourself so you will know what you are doing correctly and incorrectly. Knowing your strong and weak points will allow you to work on your game with a definite purpose. This knowledge will save you some valuable time and effort.

I will help you develop self-awareness by describing the characteristics of an ideal finish—how you should look and how you should feel at the completion of your swing.

Proper footwork

Golfers can learn much about their own swings by noting their feet at the finish of their swings. Do you finish like Tom Kite (facing page)—on the outside of your left foot, with your left knee still slightly flexed and your right foot up on the toe? Or do you finish stiff-legged and relatively flat-footed like the 18-handicap amateur shown above? If the latter is true, study the text of this chapter, especially Point No. 2 of the Finish Position Checkpoints.

I'll use this approach because the way you finish your swing is directly determined by how you hold the club, set up to the ball and actually swing.

Compare your finish to this ideal, note any variations between the two and consider the reasons, which I will give you, for the variation. Then use these reasons as clues to the ways you can most directly improve your swing.

Reading this chapter and studying the photos should also improve your general understanding of what causes what in the golf swing. This understanding will help guide you in the future when seeking a cure for a specific problem.

In addition, a close study of this chapter will summarize for you the modern swing principles that I've previously made about the Square-to-Square Method.

I suggest you analyze your finish position only after actually striking golf balls. The way we finish on actual shots often differs considerably from the way we finish our practice swings.

Finish position checkpoints

1. Over-all body position: At the finish of your swing, is your body almost vertical, like the letter "I", or are you bowed forward in the "Reverse C" position, with your head well back and your forward knee well ahead of where the ball had rested? The "Reverse C" position is ideal. It indicates that your legs have properly led your shoulders on your forward swing, that your knees have "flung your arms." The "I" position suggests that too much shoulder tension has caused your upper body to move past the ball. If you find yourself in the "I" position, check to see that your grip is light at address and your shoulders loose. Play the ball off your left heel. Cock your chin toward your right shoulder before swinging. Swing your arms freely going back; lead with your left knee when swinging forward. Keep both knees flexed throughout. Swing THROUGH the ball and TO the target, not merely AT the ball.

2. Weight distribution: You should finish in the "Reverse C" position and with your weight largely on the outside of your left heel. You should have rolled this ankle toward the target. You should also finish on the toe of your right foot so that the shoe-string lacing faces the ball's original position. Failure to finish with your feet in these positions indicates improper weight shifting during your swing. First check to see that 60 to 70 per cent of your weight is on the inside of your right foot at address. Keep both knees flexed throughout your swing, especially your right knee during your back-swing. Lead with your left knee on your forward swing and let your hips turn freely as a result. Let your knees fling your arms forward freely without regard for striking the ball squarely. Over-concern about making solid contact causes you to become "ball bound." You guide or steer the clubhead back to the ball, and this impairs proper weight shifting toward the target. You will not finish on the toe of your right foot.

3. Forward-leg position: No longer is "hit against a firm left side" a Golden Rule of golf instruction. In the modern swing we hit WITH the left side, not AGAINST it. Your left knee should remain flexed through impact. If it stiffens prior to impact, your forward-swing sequence of movement does not follow the modern ideal. As a general rule, your shoulders are dominating. To reduce shoulder tension, work on a light grip and a free arm swing going back. Start your forward swing with your left knee actively sliding toward the target and your shoulders following passively behind. Striving for extra distance may also be a reason you are top-heavy. Try cutting back a few yards on full shots. I doubt that you'll actually sacrifice any distance. You may even add both distance and accuracy.

4. Left-wrist position: Are you still in the Square Position, with the back of your left hand, wrist and forearm in a straight-line relationship until near the finish of your swing? Or does your left wrist cup inward prior to or during impact? It no doubt does if you find it cupped at the finish of your swing

on chip shots. Remember that in the pulling swing we need left-hand control—as indicated by the Square Position—well past impact. Inward cupping of the back of the wrist indicates too much right-side pressure on the back side of the clubshaft during your downswing. This pressure can result from swinging on too flat a plane during your backswing or from lifting the club abruptly during the takeaway. Establish your Square Position either at address or early in your backswing, and then set your angle with the last three fingers of your left hand. Retain your angle on your forward swing by pulling with these three fingers as your knees slide toward the target. Swing your arms freely through impact and beyond so that the clubface rotates a full 180 degrees throughout your forward swing. You'll find that after making a shot a large majority of touring professionals let go of the club with their right hand first, a further indication of left-hand control throughout the swing.

5. Hands position: Your hands should swing high, well above your shoulders, as you near the finish of your swing. This results from a proper address position, the establishment of left-hand control early in your backswing and passive shoulders on your forward swing. If your hands never move higher than shoulder height, your shoulders are laboring during your forward swing. First check your aiming of the clubface and your

Finish high

Ben Crenshaw's hands swing high during his follow-through largely because of his good address position, strong left-hand control throughout his backswing and forward swing, and a proper sequence of movement—legs leading, shoulders following—during his downswing. Readers whose hands finish low like the amateur shown above-right are top-heavy during the downswing. They should study Point No. 5 of the Finish Position Checkpoints in this chapter for clues to causes of their top-heaviness.

Finish square

Not all golfers, even professionals, have sufficient left-hand control to maintain the straight-line Square Position to the finish of their swings. Jack Nicklaus can, as shown in the photo at left. The amateur below reflects the extreme result of right-hand throwing during the forward swing. Note the breakdown of his left wrist. Readers who finish in such a position will benefit greatly from the Square-to-Square drills in Chapter 7.

body alignment at address. During your takeaway, start the clubhead straight back from the ball for several inches as you set your angle with the last three fingers of your left hand. Make sure your left knee leads and your legs fling your arms freely on your forward swing. Maintain a consistently light, right-hand grip pressure throughout.

6. Arms position: You should finish your swing with your elbows about the same distance apart as they were at address. If they are farther apart, you probably haven't swung them freely throughout your swing. You should stress swinging them freely THROUGH the ball. Let your right hand rotate freely over your left as you follow through, but continue to retain the Square Position and left-hand control.

The "reverse C" position

To finish in the "Reverse C" body position shown by professional Sandra Haynie on the facing page, a player must lead with the legs and follow with the shoulders on the forward swing. If this ideal sequence is reversed—shoulders dominate legs—you will probably finish in the "I" position of the amateurs shown at left. The "Reverse C" position indicates proper pulling during the downswing. The "I" position suggests shoving. Readers who finish in the "I" position should study the text of this chapter, especially Point No. 1 of the Finish Position Checkpoints.

7.
HOW TO LEARN AND APPLY THE METHOD

Knowledge alone cannot dramatically improve your golf game. Many golfers delude themselves into searching for one secret thought that will turn them into a low-handicap player before next Saturday's game. No way! If knowledge alone could produce birdies and pars, the practice tees at pro tournaments would be empty. All the boys would be back in the room reading books such as this.

This chapter is about how to translate the knowledge I've given you in the preceding six into better shots, first on the practice tee, then on the course itself.

I believe there is a definite four-stage process of learning that all serious golfers should follow. The first is the Conceptual Stage wherein you learn what makes a golf swing succeed or fail. Thus far in this book I've dealt largely with concepts. I've presented a model method. I would hope that you have studied the text and the pictures and established certain goals or priorities that will bring you closer to this model.

The second stage of learning is the Training Stage wherein you should, through practice and drills, train your muscles to act in ways to achieve the goals you established during Stage One. This Training Stage is really a re-training period. You will teach yourself new and better swing habits to replace inferior habits. If during Stage One you decided to improve your setup, in Stage Two you will mentally direct yourself to establish and maintain this position as you practice.

Stage Three is the Internalizing Stage. During this stage you should gradually develop a self-awareness of how your new swing moves feel. You would, for example, internalize the feeling of aligning your shoulders parallel to the target line so you could do so unconsciously.

Stage Four is the Playing Stage. This takes place on the course as you translate your new swing or setup into better shots and lower scores.

See your shot before you swing

Most golfers who are learning new techniques will play poorly on the course until the new foreign positions and swing moves begin to feel comfortable. Until that time the conscious mental application needed to develop the new methods is likely to inhibit free swinging. Improved play will occur once this conscious application becomes automatic, once it's transferred to the golfer's subconscious. To speed this transfer of new techniques to muscle memory, develop "target orientation." Make it a habit on every shot to first select your target and then visualize beforehand how your shot should look flying toward it. Your subconscious mind will "develop" the last "picture" you give it before you swing. If the picture you give it is POSITIVE, if it's a "photo" of a successful shot, your chances of swinging freely with relatively little inhibition and tension will be increased.

SQUARE-TO-SQUARE GOLF IN PICTURES

These four stages overlap. Even in reading this book—a Stage One function—you probably have already begun to internalize how it will feel to make a certain swing movement—a Stage Three function. Certainly this internalizing, this growing self-awarenes of certain feelings, will occur during Stage Two, the Training Stage, and continue to grow during Stage Four, the Playing Stage.

The reason for breaking down the learning process into these four stages is that you will play your best golf only after you can swing properly WITHOUT THINKING ABOUT HOW TO SWING. Conscious mental direction of how to swing the club stifles freedom of movement and inhibits tempo and rhythm. Conscious direction is necessary during the learning stage as you develop proper swing habits, but once developed consciously these habits must be executed unconsciously on the course. Thus our end goal in learning is to train our subconscious to react automatically and produce the type of shot we may need on the course.

The Training Stage is never-ending. I'm sure that even Jack Nicklaus is still trying to refine certain moves in his swing. But even the expert plays his best on the course only when he's reached the point that he can direct his subconscious to react and apply his training automatically.

The expert golfer triggers his subconscious to respond in one or more of three ways. One way is to summon forth a certain feeling. The player looks at his target, looks at his ball, visualizes how the ball should look flying to the target, and then senses how he should feel as he swings to make the shot he's visualized. He may rehearse this feeling with one or more practice swings. During his actual swing he tries to duplicate the feeling he's sensed beforehand.

A second way to trigger the subconscious is with a swing image. Again, the player looks at his target and the ball, and visualizes the shot. However, instead of sensing how his swing should feel, he imagines how it should look. He pictures himself or some other player, say Jack Nicklaus, swinging. He then proceeds to swing like his "picture." The picture he has in mind triggers his subconscious to produce that type of swing.

The third way that experts trigger the subconscious is with a key thought. The player again determines his target, looks at the ball and visualizes the shot. Next he determines what one key thing in his swing will, if properly executed, trigger his subconscious to produce the over-all stroke he desires.

These three ways to trigger the subconscious represent the nth degree of learning you should seek as you take the concepts of this book, develop and apply them through drills and practice, and build self-awareness of how a proper grip, setup and swing actually feel.

Educators who teach motor skills have convinced me that golf instruction, to an inordinate degree, stresses how to SWING rather than how to PLAY. The Square-to-Square Method is a way to swing. But only by translating this method into actual play on the course can you improve. This process entails the four stages of learning—conceptualizing, training, internalizing and playing.

The conceptual stage

After studying the text and the photos presented so far, I hope you have a clear understanding of the goals and techniques of the Square-to-Square Method. I hope I've related with clarity why it is important to apply a pulling action on the clubshaft and how to do it.

If you have not already done so, I'd like you to review the preceding chapters and decide on your grip, setup and swing areas that need the most work. Establish a list of priorities that you will tackle during the Training Stage. List these priorities in order of importance, bearing in mind that proper grip and setup are the foundation of a proper swing.

Take the first priority on your list and further study the text and photos related to it. Do the same with the second priority only

after you have passed through the Training and Internalizing Stages of learning the first.

The training stage

During this period you will exchange old habits for new ones. In practice sessions you will be using ''foreign'' muscles in foreign ways. You will be mentally directing yourself to do something that may feel uncomfortable for a time. Not only will you feel uncomfortable, but your shots may not come off as well as they have in the past. You may become discouraged. You may be tempted to discard that which feels foreign and revert to that which feels comfortable. Many students drop out at this stage.

I mention this possible discouragement not to worry you, but to help you cope with it. You should understand that during the Training Stage you will not only be using new muscles new ways, but also you will be working with parts of your swing. Segmenting the swing into various pieces temporarily may inhibit the swing as a whole. With practice the new part will gradually blend into, and improve your whole stroke.

As you concentrate on improving parts of your swing, it will lose some of its grace and fluidity. Ask someone to write his name on a piece of paper. Then ask him to copy it, trying to duplicate every curl and dip of every letter in the first signature. You'll find the second name lacks the freedom, flow and abandon of the first. The lines will appear thicker, reflecting added pressure. This test shows how mental direction inhibits motion. Therefore, as you think consciously about various parts of your swing, constantly try to maintain an over-all feeling of smooth tempo.

As you work on segments of your swing, you will find yourself summoning forth in your mind's eye what we call "part-swing images." You will visualize a certain position—say your hands at the top of your swing—or a certain pattern of movement. The clearer these images are in your mind's eye, the easier it will be for you to duplicate them. Studying the pictures in this book will help clarify these images.

The drills that appear at the end of this chapter are designed to help you master various aspects of the Square-to-Square swing. Many can be executed at home and will shorten your Training Stage.

From the start of the Training Stage, it is vital that you begin to direct yourself toward becoming "target oriented." Many golfers spend their lives on the practice tee perfecting their swings, but never fully benefit from their efforts in terms of lower scores. They become so consumed with swing thoughts that they lose sight of the purpose of the swing: to project the ball to a specific target.

Earlier I mentioned three ways expert golfers trigger the subconscious. In each case they first select a target and visualize the ball going to it. This gives their subconscious a positive picture of what it must do during the swing. Once proper swing habits are developed during the Training Stage and absorbed during the Internalizing Stage, your subconscious is programmed to produce a free, smooth, proper swing without much mental direction. However, without a clear image of the target and the shot you intend to play, your subconscious cannot take over to produce the results you seek.

Developing target orientation during the Training Stage also takes your mind off the ball. Most golfers are overly concerned about striking the ball squarely. This concern inhibits free swinging as they try to guide and steer the clubhead squarely back to the ball. The fear of mis-hitting the ball breeds both mental and physical tension that produces bad swings. Over-concern about the ball also produces bad swings because sub-consciously we tend to swing AT it, rather than THROUGH it. Our legs and left arm slow down. Our throwing hand takes over and we lose our angle too early.

In short, developing target orientation during the Training Stage will (1) minimize the tensions inherent in learning new moves that feel foreign, (2) train you to hold specific goals in your subconscious when you later play the course and (3) train you to relate arm speed and motion with specific distances.

During the Training Stage, I suggest you hit balls with a short iron, say a 7-iron. I also suggest you tee the ball at first. During this period of learning, we are trying to build success patterns—solid shots—and experience how it feels to make them so that later we can recapture that feeling during actual play. We are trying to make new moves properly and also trying to build confidence in them. Gradually you can lower the ball on the tee peg until it is at ground level.

Finally, during each training session you should check your grip, aim and setup. If these are incorrect, you will tend to make bad shots and blame your new swing moves for creating them. Don't let pre-swing faults cause you to discard proper swing habits.

The internalizing stage

This stage of learning takes place almost concurrently with the Training Stage. As you gradually master the priorities you have set for yourself, you should learn to sense how each feels.

At first you probably will be training yourself to make only a segment of your swing properly. Or you may be working on your grip or your setup position. You will absorb a self-awareness of only part of your swing. You will, for instance, become aware of how it feels to be set up properly. Though this feeling may be uncomfortable at first, you should nevertheless absorb it.

Learn to identify the feeling of proper grip, setup and swing parts until they begin to feel normal. Then learn to repeat these priorities by recalling how they should feel, rather than through conscious mental direction of how your body and the club should move.

At this stage you should be more concerned about what you feel as you swing than about shot results. Strive constantly to produce the swing image you have in mind AND to sense how it feels to produce that image.

Also you should develop the habit of relating the results of your shots to the feeling of your swing. Most golfers relate shot results to the feeling of impact when the clubhead contacts the ball. You should also relate your shots to the feeling of the swing that produced them. As you develop this habit during your practice sessions, you will gradually learn to sense how it feels to make the type of swing that produces a hook, slice, high fade, and other types of shots. Then, during your Playing Stage, you will be able to "feel" beforehand the type of swing you will need to produce the shot you need.

Gradually internalizing the sensations of proper swinging will also help you in the future when your swing goes sour. Recalling these sensations will help you overcome the fault that is causing the problem.

The playing stage

During the Training and Internalizing Stages, you develop proper swing habits and learn to identify them by feel. You do this on the practice tee until foreign positions and movements start to feel normal. Then you build success patterns from this feel.

On the course, you will play your best when you first orient yourself to the target, visualize the shot you want to play and then trigger your subconscious to produce the swing needed for the shot in question. You will trigger your subconscious to play its role by first showing it how your shot should look and then telling it (1) how your swing should feel or (2) how it should look or (3) what key move it should allow you to make, or a combination of the three.

If you happen to be playing by feel on a given shot, you will sense how your over-all swing should feel to make that shot. If you have trained yourself properly and internalized properly in practice, you will be able to sense this over-all swing feeling for the shot in question even before you set up to the ball. You may want to rehearse this feeling during your practice swing. If you continue to sense how your swing should feel as you set up to the ball, subconsciously you will adjust your setup to help produce that swing.

If you are triggering your subconscious on the course with a certain swing image, you will tell it beforehand how you want your swing to look. You will give your subconscious a picture of your swing, or the swing of another player. Thereafter you will merely let your subconscious help you "develop" the photo you have in your mind's eye as you swing.

If you are playing a shot with a key thought in mind—say, to finish with your hands high—you will sense beforehand how it will feel to make that thought happen, or you will visualize yourself executing that thought.

Expert golfers have a variety of key thoughts, swing images and over-all swing sensations. During pre-round practice sessions they search for the particular thought, image or swing sensation that seems to produce the best results on that particular day. Whichever they choose to play with that day may not work the next day. Our metabolism changes from day to day and good players learn to find the key thought, swing image or over-all swing sensation that best suits their needs on any given day, any given stage of a round, or even on a given shot.

Certain things remain constant, however. One is the need to orient yourself to a target on every shot. You must establish your goal and this goal always must be somewhere in the distance, never the ball at your feet.

The second thing that remains constant in golf is that you will play best when you are relatively free of mental and physical tension. Tension inhibits free swinging. Concern about striking the ball squarely produces tension. Look at the ball but think "target." Negative thoughts produce tension. Visualize a successful shot as you prepare to swing and while swinging. Too many swing thoughts confuse your subconscious and produce physical tension. Try to direct your thinking towards one over-all swing feel, one clear swing image or one key thought.

A third constant is that thoughts involving backswing positions generally restrict freedom of movement; forward swing thoughts encourage free swinging. If you play with a key thought while swinging, choose a thought that involves your forward swing. If you play with a swing image in mind, it's better to "see" your finish position than to visualize your position at the top of your backswing. Also, thoughts involving key movements are generally less inhibiting than thoughts about key positions.

A fourth constant is the course itself. It's there before you. It's inanimate. It's waiting to challenge you. Your attitude should be that you are going to meet this challenge with confidence in your ability. If the course beats you on one shot or on one hole, feel confident that you'll beat it on the next. If your ball finishes in a divot mark, don't bemoan your bad luck. Instead, determine how you will "get back" at the course with your next shot. Visualize the shot you'll play. Play it confidently.

The fifth and final constant I'd like to mention is the fact that your game was, is and always will be imperfect. I feel that no golfer will duplicate the model I have presented in this book on every shot. In golf, learning is truly never-ending. I suggest you strive to master the Square-to-Square Method because it incorporates the best principles of the modern golf swing, but accept that you will not achieve perfection on every shot. If you make a mistake, play on from there as best you can. Once you accept this philosophy, you'll enjoy this wonderful game more, and you'll play it better.

Drills

The drills that follow, illustrated by photos of me, are designed specifically to help you apply techniques of the Square-to-Square Method. Performing the drills will strengthen the muscles you'll use in the golf swing that stress pulling, rather than throwing, shoving or pushing the club. It will also impart to you the sensations you should feel when swinging Square-to-Square. Internalize these sensations as you perform the drills and you will greatly shorten the learning process described in this chapter.

DRILLS

Build motion first

Freedom of movement is vital to any golf swing, but especially Square-to-Square. The drill shown here is designed to produce such motion. Simply swing your arms freely back and through several times as shown in the photos. Strive for complete freedom from arm and shoulder tension. Let your swinging arms turn your shoulders, not vice versa. As you swing forward, make sure your legs lead the way. Feel them fling your arms. Feel yourself roll onto the outside of your left foot and onto the toe of your right. YOU SHOULD NOT PROGRESS WITH THE SQUARE-TO-SQUARE METHOD UNTIL YOU CAN FINISH IN THE "REVERSE C" POSITION AS YOU EXECUTE THIS DRILL. Further freedom of arm swinging can be achieved by hitting iron shots—preferably with the ball teed—and with your feet together. If you hit the ball more squarely with your feet together than on normal shots, your normal shots need a freer arm swing.

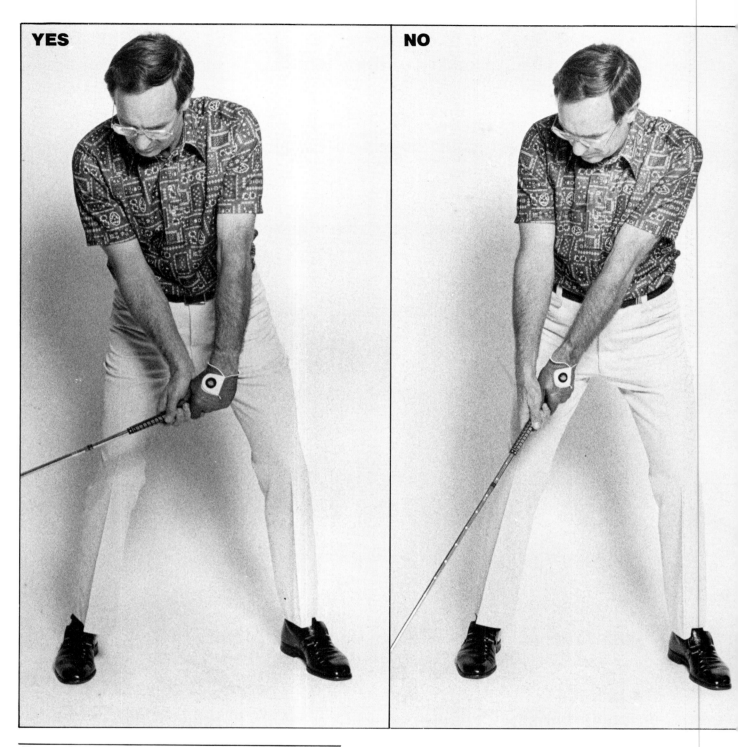

YES

NO

Develop your waggle

The Square-to-Square swing requires a relatively passive
right hand and arm throughout. For most golfers this
passiveness must be cultivated. Learning to waggle
correctly will teach you to establish proper left-hand
dominance. Practice waggling the clubhead back from the
ball with the last three fingers of your left hand as I am
doing in the photo on the left. Maintain a light grip pressure
in your right hand as you do so. Let your left hand break
down the tension in your right wrist and arm. Avoid pulling
the club back with the right arm and hand as I am doing in
the photo on the right. Gradually build this waggle into
your actual shotmaking as you practice.

Build left hand-arm strength

The muscles that help pull the clubshaft down and forward in the Square-to-Square swing are those in the last three fingers of the left hand and the underside of the left forearm. Hold a club in front of you with this hand and rotate it back and forth as I am doing in these photos. Don't let the back of your wrist cup inward. Choke down on the clubshaft if you do not have enough strength to do this at first. Practice this drill at least twice daily until your arm tires. This drill not only gives you the strength you need to swing Square-to-Square, but also helps develop the proper forearm rotation that I describe in Chapter 5.

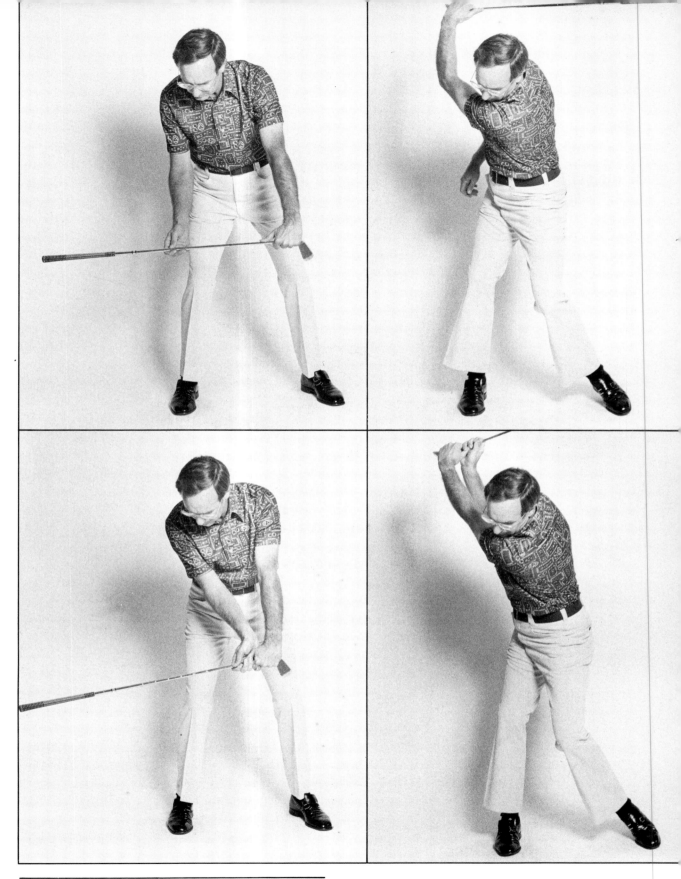

Create "swish"

The Square-to-Square swing requires that your legs, left arm and left hand pull the clubshaft on your forward swing. This drill is designed to develop this ability to pull and to de-emphasize any tendency you might have to throw or shove with your right hand, arm and side. First, hold an iron club with your left hand on the head end of the shaft and swing it back and forward as I'm doing in the top photos. Listen for the "swish" sound of the clubshaft. Next, put both hands on the club and repeat the drill. If you don't hear as much swish, you are over-controlling the club with your right hand, arm and shoulder. Lighten your right-hand grip, relax your right arm and lead with your legs on your downswing. Once you can make the swish with both hands on the club,

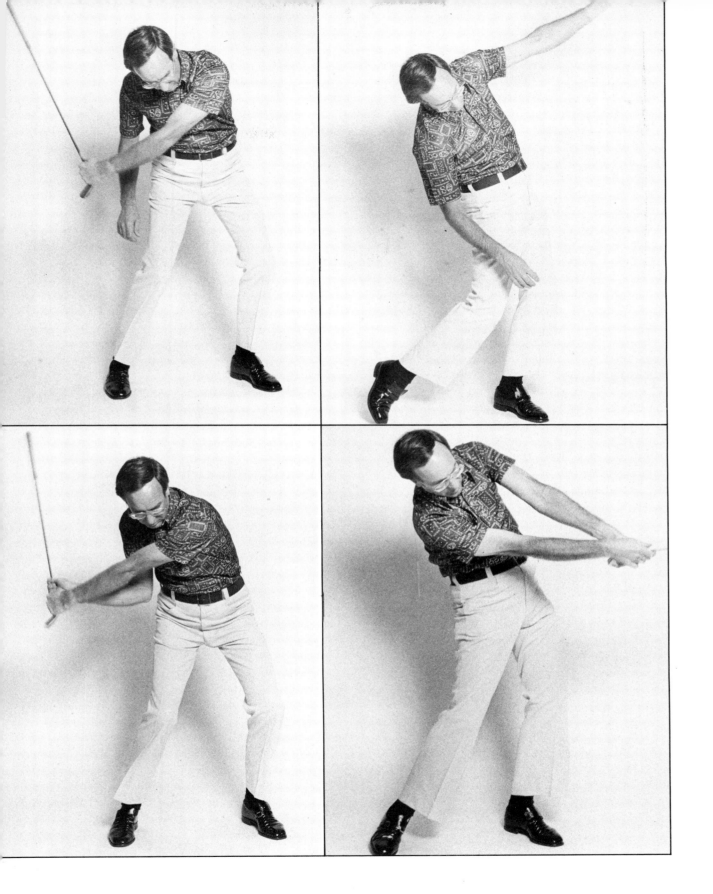

apply this same light right-hand grip, free arm swing and leg drive on your regular shots. Another good drill to reduce right-hand influence is to hit shots while gripping the club with your right forefinger resting atop instead of below the shaft. As you hit shots with this grip, sense how actively the last three fingers of your left hand control the club.

Swing Square-to-Square — one-handed

The best over-all drill for developing Square-to-Square golf muscles is simply to apply the techniques described in this book to a stroke in which you hold the club only in your left hand. Be sure you establish the straight-line Square Position either at address or early in your backswing as you set your angle. Thereafter try to maintain it through to the finish of your swing. Lead with your legs on your forward swing. Let them fling your arm. Rotate the clubshaft counterclockwise with the last three fingers and forearm as you swing it through the hitting area. Try to finish with your hand high, your body in the "Reverse C" position and your weight on the outside of your left foot.

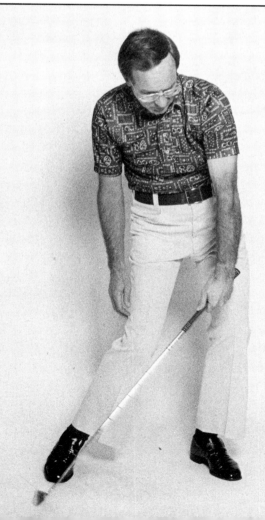

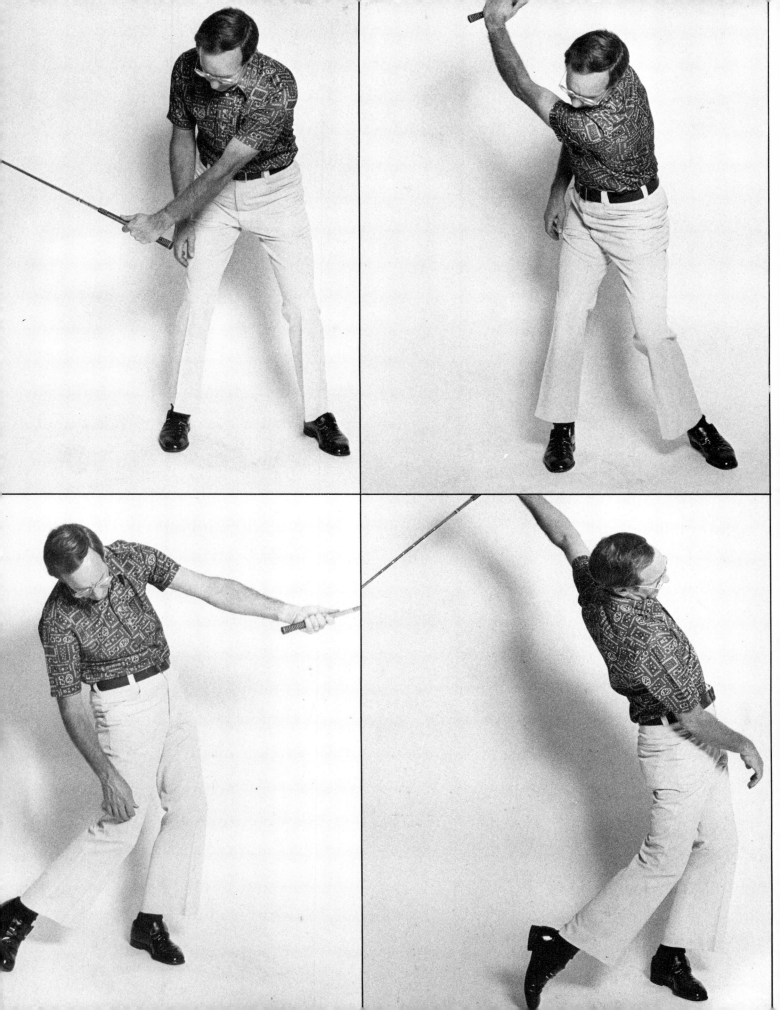

PHOTOGRAPH CREDITS

Joe Bilbao—pp. 39, 91; Chuck Brenkus—20, 26-27, 58;
Bruce Curtis—39, 92, 99, 102, 105, 108; Walt Disney Productions
—113; Jeff Fox—10-11; Frank Gardner—58, 59; Howard Gill—
94-95; Golf Digest staff—39; Leonard Kamsler—12-19, 22-23,
24, 30-31, 32-35, 39, 42-43, 44-45, 48-49, 52-53, 57, 62-85, 87,
88-89, 92, 93, 96, 97, 99, 100-101, 102, 104, 108, 109, 111;
John P. May—56, 96; Bill Mount—58, 98; Lester Nehamkin—
20, 110; John Newcomb—21; Owens-Corning Fiberglas
Corporation—59; Mike Ronman—99; Al Satterwhite—21;
Barry Tenin—21; Peter Travers—59; Ed Vebell—28-29, 120-127;
J. Wager—99.

Photographs of Jack Nicklaus, pp. 62-85, 92, and 109,
published by arrangement with SportsConcepts Inc.

Photographs of Tommy Bolt, pp. 32-35, 87 and 96,
Bruce Crampton, 24, 88-89, and Lee Trevino, 24, courtesy of
Sports Marketing, Inc.

Designer: John Newcomb
Art assistants: Laura Duggan, John Kennedy